The Life Beyond the Veil Volume I

The Lowlands of Heaven

The Life Beyond the Veil series consists of five volumes:

The Lowlands of Heaven
The Highlands of Heaven
The Ministry of Heaven
The Battilions of Heaven
The Outlands of Heaven

Spirit Messages received and set down by the Rev. George Vale Owen. (1860-1931) Vicar of Orford, Lancashire, England.

ISBN.: **978-1-329-80558-3**

The Life Beyond the Veil
Volume I

The Lowlands of Heaven

LONDON

PRINTED IN THE UNITED KINGDOM.

This volume was printed in June 1920, April 1926, April 1929, March 1945, Sept 1947 and July 1949. It was also printed in the U.S.A.

This print version was created by Geoff Cutler in August 2015 and no copyright is claimed in this publication. This edition contains the preface from both the first 1920 edition and the revised 1949 edition, as I found that there is slightly different information contained in each. Obviously the reader can simply skip one of these if they have little interest in the background of Rev. George Vale Owen.

THE REV. G. VALE OWEN

VICAR OF ORFORD, LANCS.,
1908-1922

The Rev. George Vale Owen, Vicar of Orford from 1908 to 1922.

THE CHURCH OF ST. MARGARET & ALL HALLOWS, ORFORD, WARRINGTON, LANCASHIRE, OF WHICH THE REV. G. VALE OWEN IS THE INCUMBENT

× The Vestry referred to on p. xxi.

The Church of St. Margaret and All Hallows, Orford, Warrington, Lancashire, England.

Table of Contents

Foreword (1949)

The Greater World Association have undertaken to reprint the four volumes comprising the illuminating Scripts received through the mediumship of the Rev. G. Vale Owen. It has been a great loss to the Movement that these books have been out of print for so long, for it is generally agreed that no other communications from Spirit Realms have had such a wide appeal to the world at large. This is due partly, we know, to the extensive publicity given to them by that great newspaper Proprietor, Lord Northcliffe, who, ignoring general prejudice and cynicism regarding the possibility of such communications, published them serially in The WEEKLY DESPATCH in 1920-21, and spent a great deal of money in announcing their appearance.

It is natural to ask: "How were these Spirit Messages received?" The answer is given by Vale Owen himself in the first book of the series. The Lowlands of Heaven.

Then comes the next question: "What was this clergyman like?" Those who did not meet Vale Owen might well picture a dreamer, a man separated from the usual things of daily life—a saint or an ascetic. But although all who knew Vale Owen personally had no doubt about his spirituality, they would not agree that he was a man who "lived in the clouds"; rather he was one who needed human love and the gladness of physical life.

We are very grateful, therefore, to the Rev. G. Eustace Owen for giving us a few details about his father which shows that he was a practical man with a sense of humour and a great tolerance for the weakness of others, which means that he was a very good companion as well as a good Christian. The Rev. Eustace Owen writes :

"In his book WITH NORTHCLIFFE IN FLEET STREET, J. A. Hammerton alludes to the Rev. Vale Owen as 'that typical visionary of the half-Christian, half-spiritualist sort.' That view is held by many people who knew him through his writings; but it is not a true portrait. My father was a visionary without being a crank. While having a clear view of life's spiritual basis, he was most practical and methodical in all his ways.

"I remember how gently he dealt with others, how broad-minded he was in argument, his tolerance of opponents, and how he endured persecution with immense patience. Many an opponent's sword was blunted by his understanding of the one who wielded it! Yet he could be severe when necessary. Cruelty in any form roused his indignation. To bullies and schemers he became a very Elijah!

"I have never known anyone more direct in thought and words, or one who so detested shams. Beneath his graciousness lay the hardness of a good soldier of the Cross, so that he bore scorn and persecution without wavering. Quietness sometimes conceals a rare courage.

"In the book HE LAUGHED IN FLEET STREET, Bernard Falk describes a meeting between Lord Northcliffe and my father, in 'The Times' office, when the former asked him to accept £1,000 for publishing extracts from the Script in the 'Weekly Despatch.'

"He continues:

'Vale Owen shook his head. For this part of his writings, he said, he could not take any money. He had been well paid by the publicity given him, and by being able to carry out the sacred duty of placing his revelations before the world. Knowing well Vale Owen's poverty I was genuinely sorry to hear him refuse payment, but he was not to be dissuaded. .

The Rev. G. Eustace Owen adds :

"All our family are pleased that the Script is not to be allowed to remain in oblivion. The rising generation particularly need the comfort and illumination of its message. We are all so glad that 'The Greater World' have so keenly and so boldly taken up this re-publication. May their confidence be justified and their labours blessed!"

An Appreciation

By Lord Northcliffe[1]

I have not had an opportunity of reading the whole of The Life Beyond the Veil, but among the passages I have perused are many of great beauty.

It seems to me that the personality of the Rev. G. Vale Owen is a matter of deep importance and to be considered in connection with these very remarkable documents. During the brief interview that I had with him I felt that I was in the presence of a man of sincerity and conviction. He laid no claims to any particular psychic gift. He expressed a desire for as little publicity as possible, and declined any of the great emoluments that could easily have come to him as the result of the enormous interest felt by the public all over the world in these scripts.

---

[1] Lord Northcliffe owned the newspaper 'The Weekly Despatch', and over the period 1920 to 1921 serialised these communications. This created enormous public interest, the vast majority of it was very favourable, and Rev. George Vale Owen was even asked to go down to London to deliver a sermon on them. There did not appear to be any significant theological objections from the Church of England, and in fact it was accepted that these communications were genuine "inspirational writings", that the Rev. G. Vale Owen was genuine, and that the writings were of great value. In spite of this they have all but disappeared from sight today. G.J.C.

Preface (1921)

THIS volume contains the first of a series of communications from beyond the veil, received and written down by the Rev. G. Vale Owen, Vicar of Orford, Lancashire.

It should be clearly understood that these messages, while complete in themselves, deal chiefly with the "Sphere of Light" nearest to the Earth in which the Vicar's mother, who is the principal communicator, states that she dwells, and that her impressions are chiefly individual to herself and are thus those of a newcomer and learner whose experiences are limited to a restricted area. Wider regions and greater heights and depths are explored, the inter-relation of this and the after-life is more fully explained, and both narrative and exposition of aims and principles are more vigorous, clear and comprehensive in succeeding messages, contained in other volumes of the series which follow this.

That said, however, the high importance and far-reaching significance of this volume must be affirmed. It gives the most complete and most detailed statement of conditions in the after-life yet published. It must be read and studied in order to gain an understanding of the further messages.

The narrative brings one face to face with a Spiritual Universe of unimaginable immensity and grandeur, with sphere upon sphere of the realms of light which stretch away into infinity. We are told that those who have passed from our earth life inhabit the nearer spheres, amid surroundings not wholly dissimilar from those they have known in this world; that at death we shall enter the sphere for which our spiritual development fits us. There is to be no sudden change in our personality. We shall not be plunged into forgetfulness. A human being is not transformed into another being.

In the first sphere of light we find trees and flowers like those that grow in earthly gardens; but more beautiful, immune from decay and death, and endowed with qualities that make them more completely a part of our lives. Around us are birds and animals, still the friends of man, but nearer, more intelligent, and freed from the fears and the cruelties they suffer here.

We find houses and gardens, but of substance, colour and atmosphere more responsive to our presence; water whose playing is music; wide-ranging harmonies of colour. We find everything more radiant, more joyous, more exquisitely complex, and while our activities are multiplied, our life is more restful.

Differences in age disappear. There, are no "old" in the Spheres of Light; there are only the graceful and strong.

Spirits from a higher sphere may descend to the lower, may even be sent on a mission to Earth. But ere they can reach us they must first accustom themselves to the dimmer light and heavier "air" of the lower spheres. They must undergo a change ere they can penetrate the dense and murky atmosphere in which our world is enfolded.

That is why the spirit voices so often reach us in broken fragments which our dull intelligence can hardly piece together. That is why we can so rarely hear the words and feel the presence of those who are longing to reach and to comfort their friends.

So small a thing is the change which we call death, the narrative tells us, that many do not realize it. They have to be taught that they are in another world, the world of reunion. "She fell asleep," says one of the messages which describe the passing of such a spirit: "she fell asleep, and the cord of life was severed by our watching friends, and then softly they awoke her, and she looked up and smiled very sweetly into the face of one who leaned over her.... She began to wonder why these strange faces were around her in place of the friends and nurses she had last seen.

"She inquired where she was. When she was told, a look of wonder and yearning came over her face, and she asked to be allowed to see the friends she had left.

"This was granted her, and she looked on them through the veil, and shook her head sadly. 'If only they could know,' she said, 'how free from pain I am now and comfortable! Can you not tell them?'

"We tried to do so, but only one of them heard, I think, and he only imperfectly, and soon put it away as a fancy."

To many, indeed, these spirit messages will seem to shed new illumination upon passages in the Bible whose interpretation they have hitherto regarded as obscure. Others, whose faith may have wavered beneath the impact of modern criticism or under the trials of sorrow and bereavement, may well find in this new revelation the answer that will resolve their doubts and deepen into certainty their hope of ultimate reunion after death.

Here is a document which is placed before the reader as an authentic communication from the world beyond. No man can say what the limits of its influence will be, or how far-reaching an effect it may have upon the minds and lives of the men and women by whom it will be read.

But one thing is certain. A manuscript of such a character, coming from such a source, demands the most careful study—so tremendous are the claims made for these revelations, so rich in human interest is the actual narrative, so undoubted is Mr. Vale Owen's sincerity.

G.V.O.

"What Manner of Man is he?"

The Rev. G. Vale Owen is a typical clergyman of the Church of England, devoted to his parish and completely absorbed in his work.

Nothing was further from his thoughts, a few years ago, than that he should be made a medium for "spirit" communications.

His career has been uneventful. Born in Birmingham in 1869, and educated at the Midland Institute and Queen's College in that city, he was ordained by the Bishop of Liverpool to the curacy of Seaforth in 1893; then was curate successively of Fairfield, 1895, and of Matthew's, Scotland Road, 1897—both of Liverpool.

It was in 1900 that he went to Orford, Warrington, as curate-in-charge.

Orford Church was built in 1908, when a new parish was formed and he became the first vicar. His vicarage was built so recently as 1915.

Though he feared that the quietude of his life in his parish would be disturbed, Mr. Vale Owen felt that the importance of the revelations which were sent through him did not permit him to follow his own wishes and withhold his name, and regarding himself as only an instrument for the transmission of the messages, he refused to accept any money payment for the publication of the scripts, great as had been the labour they had thrown upon him.

Though his personality was much discussed on the first appearance of the messages, that circumstance did not affect his absorption in the work of his parish. He felt that that parish was peculiarly his own, since his was the only church in the village, and he had become intimately bound up with every family in it during his twenty years' service.

Villagers speak of him as "G.V.O."—an abbreviation of his name which in itself is a sign of affection. One of them recounted an incident typical of the means by which he has won and retained their close friendship.

"Coming home late one night," he said, "I was startled to see a tall, dark figure dash past me at a run. It was our Vicar. I learnt afterwards that one of his young parishioners, who was ill, had become restless through pain, and had asked that Mr. Owen should come and talk to her and pray at her bedside. Her brother had at once cycled to the vicarage, and Mr. Owen, who had retired for the night, had dressed at top speed and hurried to the house.

"He is always available at any hour, and such is his influence that invalids belonging to all denominations ask for him. Can you wonder why he is a welcome guest in every house?"

When Mr. Vale Owen went first to Orford his congregation worshipped in a large room of the village schoolroom. He told them they were "getting their religion too cheaply" and did not appreciate it enough. Then, obtaining donations from prosperous friends of the village, he called the parishioners together and organized a system of weekly collections, to which every family subscribed according to its means. In this way he succeeded in getting a church bat and an excellent organ installed.

When the War came, about 200 Orford men served in the Forces. All of them regarded "G.V.O." as their chief "home pal" and wrote to him regularly of their adventures. All were "his lads," and he always wrote encouraging them to "play the game."

In appearance, the Rev. G. Vale Owen is tall, spare, and a little bent.

One might at first judge him to be the shy recluse. But his deeply-lined face lights up readily with a smile and, most unassuming and approachable of men, he has a genius for friendship. There is no trace of the aloofness of the dreamer in his relations with anyone with whom he comes in contact.

He is above all practical. The building of his new church at a time which many thought premature, is one of the standing evidences of that quality.

To know him is to realize that he is a fitting instrument indeed to receive such communications as are set forth in these pages. His life has been one of strenuous endeavour to help his fellows to understand the reality of sacred things, to lighten their hearts and strengthen their courage; his first thought and his last have been for others. But G.V.O.'s point of view may perhaps best be shown by the following illustration.

Amongst many thousands of letters received at the vicarage at Orford during the early days of the publication of the script in The Weekly Dispatch was this:

"Rev. Sir,—Pray for the writer of this note who is in great trouble concerning a little child who is afflicted. I have read about you and I feel you must be very near to God, and if you were to say, 'Dear Father, help your child,' He would hear. Please do not fail to pray. The Lord understands. This is a cry for help from a mother's aching heart. God bless you."

Mr. Vale Owen's comment in speaking of this to a friend was:

"...And yet The Weekly Dispatch says I am receiving no payment."

It was in this spirit that the Vicar of Orford gave permission for these communications to be placed before the world. He hoped that by so doing he would be instrumental in bringing light into many dark places, strengthening the faith of the people and doing his humble duty to those fair angel friends, who, as he himself often remarked, "have been so gentle and patient with me during those precious hours I spent at their bidding in the vestry of the little Parish Church at Orford."

H. W. ENGHOLM.
LONDON.
May, 1920.

General Notes

How the Messages Came

IN the typewritten copies of the original manuscript, Mr. Vale Owen gave a description of how it came about that he acted as amanuensis for his mother and the spirit beings who in turn took her place at the sittings in the vestry of the church at Orford.

He said:

"There is an opinion abroad that the clergy are very credulous beings. But our training in the exercise of the critical faculty places us among the most hard-to-convince when any new truth is in question. It took a quarter of a century to convince me—ten years that spirit communication was a fact, and fifteen that the fact was legitimate and good.

"From the moment I had taken this decision, the answer began to appear. First my wife developed the power of automatic writing. Then through her I received requests that I would sit quietly, pencil in hand, and take down any thoughts which seem to come into my mind projected there by some external personality and not consequent on the exercise of my own mentality. Reluctance lasted a long time, but at last I felt that friends were at hand who wished very earnestly to speak with me. They did not overrule or compel my will in any way—that would have settled the matter at once, so far as I was concerned—but their wishes were made ever more plain.

"I felt at last that I ought to give them an opportunity, for I was impressed with the feeling that the influence was a good one, so, at last, very doubtfully I decided to sit in my cassock in the vestry after Evensong.

"The first four or five messages wandered aimlessly from one subject to another. But gradually the sentences began to take consecutive form, and at last I got some which were understandable. From that time, development kept pace with practice. When the whole series of messages was finished I reckoned up and found that the speed had been maintained at an average rate of twenty-four words a minute. On two occasions only had I any idea what subject was to be treated. That was when the message had obviously been left uncompleted. At other times I had fully expected a certain subject to be taken, but on taking up

my pencil the stream of thought went off in an altogether different direction.
"G. V. O."

How the Communicators Operated on the Other Side

It is particularly interesting to note the explanations given by his mother and others of their methods of impressing the mind of Mr. Vale Owen with the words they wished his hand to write. We select the following illustrative passages, which, however, do not appear in this, the first, volume of communications.

It transpired from a later script that when Mr. Vale Owen's mother was communicating, the girl Kathleen, mentioned below, acted for her on the other side as an amanuensis, and controlled the actual writing down of the messages for all the communicators. In the case of Mr. Vale Owen's mother the difficulties of getting through antique words and expressions that were not modern did not, of course, arise in her case, but there seems no doubt from the character of many of her messages that she was not alone in giving them.

(Extract from a later script.)

"Only in part are we able to make in anywise clear to you the method we are employing in this particular case. And that we will so far as we be able.

"First, then, here we stand a group tonight of seven—sometimes more, at others less. We have already broadly settled what we will say to you, but leave the precise wording till we sight you and sense your disposition of mind.

"Then, we take our stand a little distance away lest our influence, the emanations of our several minds, reach you in detail, and not as one stream but as many, and so confuse you. But from the little distance at which we stand they merge and mingle, and are focused into one, so that by the time our thoughts reach you there is unity and not multiplicity of diction.

"When you sometimes hesitate, doubtful of a word or phrase, that is when our thoughts, mingling in one, are not quite perfected into the special word required. You pause: and, continuing their blending together, our thoughts at last assume unity, and then you get our idea and at once continue on your way. You have noticed this, doubtless?"

"Yes, but I did not know the cause."[2]

"No. Well, now, to continue. We think our thoughts to you, and sometimes they are in such words as are too antique, as you say, for you to grasp them readily. This is remedied by filtering them through a more modern instrument, and it is of this we now would speak. "That instrument is your little friend Kathleen,[3] who is good enough to come between you and us, and so render our thoughts available for you. This in more ways than one.

"First, because she is nearer to you in status than we, —who, having been longer here, have become somewhat removed from Earth. She is of more recent transplanting, and not yet so far away that when she speaks you cannot hear.

"For a like reason also she comes between. That is, by the words that form her present store. She can still think in her old tongue of Earth, and it is more modern than our own—though we like it not so well, since it seems to us more composite and less precise.

"But we must not find fault with what is still beautiful. We have, no doubt, still our prejudices and insularity; when we come down here we cannot but take on anew some of those traits we once had but gradually have cast aside.

"The little lady Kathleen is nearer you than we in these respects, and the stream of our impelling we direct on you through her for that reason.

"However, we stand a little apart from you, because the presence of us combined would overmatch you. You could not write down what we would give, and our purpose in coming is to give you such narrative of words as you and others may read with intelligence.

"You glance at the dial of your timekeeper. You call it a watch. Why? That is one little instance of our preference for our older way of speaking. Timekeeper seems to us more explicit than the other word. The meaning of your glance is clear, whatever we call the thing on which it fall. So we bid you good night, good friend....

---

[2] Question by G.V.O. These are in Italics.

[3] See notes on Kathleen on page xx.

"We find sometimes, when we read what message we have given, that much which we tried to impress is not apparent there, and some lesser quantity of what we had not in mind appears.

"This is but a natural consequence of the intervention of so thick a veil between the sphere from which we speak and that in which the recorder [i.e. Mr. Vale Owen] lives, his life.

"The atmosphere of the two spheres is so diverse in quality that, in passing from one to the other, there is always a diminution of speed, so sudden and so marked that a shock is given to the stream of our thoughts, and there is produced, just on the border-line, some inevitable confusion. This is one of the many difficulties we find.

"Here is another. The human brain is a very wonderful instrument, but it is of material substance, and, even when the stream of our thoughts reaches and impinges upon it, yet, because of its density, the penetration is impeded and sometimes altogether brought to a stop. For the vibrations, as they leave us, are of high intensity, and the fineness of their quality is a hindrance to their effecting a correspondence in the human brain, which is, gross by comparison.

"Once again: there are many things here for which there are no words in any of the Earth languages to express their meaning.

"There are colours which your eyes do not see, but are present in your spectrum; there are more colours which are of higher sublimity than could be reproduced by the medium, which shows both the Earth colours to you and registers those invisible to you, but present withal.

"There are also notes and tones of sound of like nature, and too fine for registration by the atmosphere of Earth.

"There are forces also, not available with you, not able, to be expressed to you….

"These and other matters are interpenetrating all our life and forming our environment. And when we come to speak of our life here, or of the causes we see in operation, of which you behold the effects alone, we are much perplexed and strive continually to find just how to say it so that it shall be both understood of you and also not too wide of a target as known to us.

"So you will see that we have a task to do in speaking into

your sphere from this of ours which is by no means easy. Still, it is worth the doing of it, and so we essay our best and try to rest content."

Mr. Vale Owen's Comments

In view of the above description, it is interesting to have the following remarks from Mr. Vale Owen, descriptive of his mental and physical condition during the time he was actually receiving the communications, In a letter to the Editor of this volume, Mr. Vale Owen wrote:

"You point out to me the fact that, while in the script itself my communicators give not a little information as to the methods employed in the transmission of messages from their side to ours, yet, on my own part, I have never given you any definite description of the effect produced upon myself.

"The effect of what, perhaps, we might term the more mechanical operations, as these impinge upon the organism of the human brain, the transmitters themselves describe in some detail. Vibrations, initiated by them and projected through the Veil, find their target in the mentality of the human instrument and are reproduced, on this side, in what is, in effect, a kind of inner clairvoyance and clairaudience. Viewed inversely, from the standpoint of the instrument himself, it assumes an aspect something like this: the scenes they describe seem to come along a kind of X-ray stream of vibrations and are received by means of the faculty of visualization. That is, he sees these scenes in his imagination as he, by a similar process, is able to visualize his garden or house, or other well-known place, when at a distance.

"The words of the messages seem to travel on a celestial-mundane telephonic current. He can hear them interiorly in much the same manner as he is able to hum over a well-remembered tune, or to reproduce a speech he has heard with all its inflections and cadences, pathetic or uplifting—all this also interiorly, and without himself uttering a sound. In addition, however, there is a deeper content in the operation. It is that effect upon the human instrument produced by the more or less intimate contact of spirit with spirit. This is actual 'Spiritual Communion,' and is recognized in the Creed of Christendom in the article 'The Communion of Saints.'

"Here enters in an essentially spiritual element which, as our spirit-communicators repeatedly tell us, it is not possible adequately to contain in any earthly form of words. It is uplifting to the boundaries, and on occasion, into the very domain, of ecstasy.

"At times such as these earth and earth's affairs retreat into the background, and glimpses are had of what eternity and infinity mean, and of the Presence of God.

"Then Christendom assumes an enlarged aspect and occupies a broader room. It is seen that the whole Church on Earth is but a small portion of the Divine Kingdom, which includes within itself, not alone all races and all systems of religion here below, but also that realm of interstellar glories and powers in the mere contemplation of which the human heart grows faint and the reaches of human imagination fade into the boundless infinities pulsating with the heart-love of the One Ineffable Light.

"It is almost needless to add that anyone who has ever experienced such contact as this has no room in his heart any more for any paltry sentiment of self-exaltation, or of spiritual pride. I know of no better teacher of humility than this realization of the smallness of the individual earth-dweller amid the myriads of those so much brighter ones who, with himself, form the one family of the Creator.

"On the other hand, the sense of security, of comrade ship, of oneness with them, and of the sweet intimacy of their love, is a sure warrant of protection to us lesser ones to whom our angel friends bend down for our uplifting. Be a man prayerful, clean-living and of a humble mind, and no danger of 'devils' can enter in between him and them.

"Sincerely your friend,
"G. VALE OWEN.

"P.S.—For all this, yet so intimate and so perfect must be the sympathy of aim and affection existing between transmitter and receiver, that whenever any thought comes through which seems to be at variance with what is true, immediately a shock is felt and the instrument faces about, as it were, with a query in his mind, which on the part of the communicator is as immediately observed and noted.

"This sympathy is quite apart from the difference in status, both in mental and spiritual capacity, between the spirit-communicator and the human instrument, and is not affected

by it. As I have said above, they 'bend down' to us, and thus bridge over any such inequality.
"G. V. O."

About Those who Communicated

Mrs. Owen, the Vicar's mother, from whom the major portion of the messages in this volume came, died on June 8, 1909 at the age of 63. She had not during her life shown any interest in the question of spirit communication.

Her life was spent at Birmingham, where her husband, at first practising as an architect and surveyor, was compelled by a breakdown in health to change his occupation to that of a chemist. She visited Orford little, and was never during her lifetime on Earth in the vestry of the church where the messages were received.

Kathleen and Ruby

Kathleen was first heard of on July 28, 1917, when, as Mrs. Vale Owen, the Vicar's wife, was using the planchette,[4] the following interchange took place, the words written being shown in ordinary, and the questions asked in italic type:

"Kathleen."

"Who is Kathleen?"

"A friend of Ruby's. Would you like to make my acquaintance?"

"Very much, if you are Ruby's friend."

"Ruby told me to come. She said she was sure you would welcome me for her sake."

("Ruby," it should be explained, was the daughter of the Rev. G. Vale Owen. She was born at Fairfield, Liverpool, on August 26, 1895, and died at the same address on November 21, 1896.)

Kathleen, in answer to questions, said she had been a seamstress, living in Walton Breck Road, Anfield, Liverpool, and had "passed over" at the age of 28, about three years before Ruby.

---

[4] A planchette is a very basic (and material) instrument used to communicate with spirit, and it is not generally used by the more advanced spirits, hence there is often some risk in its use, if low level spirits are attracted. It is not by accident that Rev. George Vale Owen was encouraged to develop the ability to use automatic writing. G.J.C.

Ruby, she said, was taken to a home where Kathleen looked after, or "mothered" her.

According to her story, the child subsequently brought her frequently to visit Mr. Vale Owen's home, under the care of a guardian. Kathleen from that time constantly came with friends when Mrs. Vale Owen was using the planchette.

Astriel

Intermingled with the messages from Mr. Vale Owen's mother, given in this volume, came others from Astriel, who had been headmaster of a school at Warwick in mid-eighteenth century. His messages touch upon religious faith, philosophical and scientific matters. They have been separated from those of Mrs. Owen and placed in their proper order at the end of this volume.

Presence Form

The meaning of the term "Presence Form," which appears in various places in this volume and for the first time in the message dated Monday, September 29, 1913, is explained in the following communication received by Mr. Vale Owen, in answer to his request that the term be defined:

"A presence form is the form in which a person becomes localized and visible in form at a distance from himself essentially. The form is not an empty sign or symbol, but is alive with, the life of the person it so manifests, action and expression being responsive to the thought, will, action and spiritual state of its original. The personality is projected and becomes visible in any place where God (or those of His angels who are so authorized) wills the manifestation to take place.

"By this method the wishes, prayers, thoughts and the whole spiritual state of any one in the Earth life, or in any of the regions of the spiritual world, may be manifested in any place or sphere at any moment which those to whom this high gift is entrusted shall will that it be so.[5]

---

[5] This sounds very similar to the phenomenon called bilocation when it involves living humans. Several Indian gurus have been reported capable of this, as was also Padre Pio amongst many others. There is another technique that I am familiar with that can be used by spirit, and it is

"A person is not always so manifested in the same presence form, which, from time to time, may be given a different aspect and take a different shape, Under whatever aspect he manifested, however, that form is, for the time being, his real self projected."

---

termed Universe Reflectivity. Given the vast size of the Universe it follows that there would be such abilities or facilities. G.J.C.

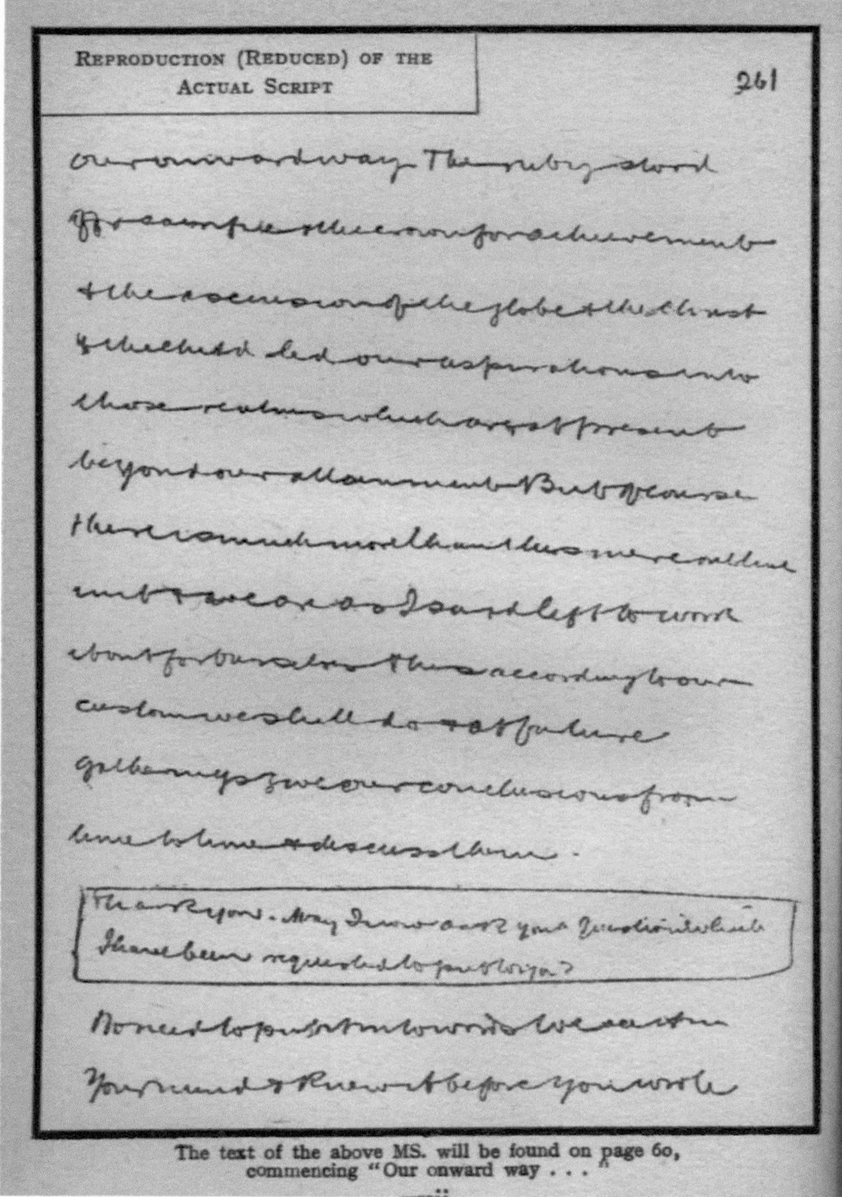

REPRODUCTION (REDUCED) OF THE ACTUAL SCRIPT

261

The text of the above MS. will be found on page 60, commencing "Our onward way . . ."

The text of the above manuscript will be found on page 37, commencing "Our onward way..."

NOTE.—Above is a reproduction of a sheet from the actual script written down by the Rev. G. Vale Owen at the sitting of October 6, 1913. It will be noticed how the words and sentences have flowed from the pencil in a swift and steady stream. They are joined together as if the writer were striving to keep pace with the communication which was being impressed upon his mind.

This page of the MS. is particularly interesting, for it shows a question written down by Mr. Vale Owen, and the answer to it immediately following in a steady flow of words.

Mr. Vale Owen always numbered a quantity of sheets of paper before he began to write. He placed these in a block before him on the table in the vestry. Then, using shaded candle-light to illuminate the sheet of paper and with his pencil in his hand, he would wait until he felt the influence to write. When once he started the influence was maintained without a stop until the message for the evening was concluded by the communicator. H. W. E.

SPECIAL NOTE.—Initials only are used throughout this volume when reference is made to any person outside Mr. Vale Owen's own family. The name Rose refers to Mr. Vale Owen's wife, and Rene is their daughter. H. W. E.

Preface (1949)

This Script—transmitted by automatic or, more correctly, by inspirational writing—falls into four distinct sections, all, however, forming one progressive whole. It was all, quite evidently, planned out in advance by those who had its transmission in hand.[6]

The link between mother and son was, no doubt, considered the most likely avenue through which to open up communication in the first instance. It was my mother, therefore, and a band of friends who transmitted to me the first part.

The experiment proving successful, another teacher was introduced named Astriel, one of higher rank and of more philosophic mind and diction. The messages given by my mother's band and Astriel form the first book of the Script, The Lowlands of Heaven.

Having passed this test I was handed over to Zabdiel, whose messages are on a higher level than the simpler narrative of my mother. These form The Highlands of Heaven.

The next phase was The Ministry of Heaven, given by one who called himself "Leader," and his band. Subsequently he seems to have assumed, more or less, sole control of communication. Then he speaks of himself as "Arnel." Under this name his narrative, which forms the fourth book, The Battalions of Heaven, is the climax of the whole. His messages are of a more intense nature than any of the foregoing, which were evidently preparatory.

It will be obvious that, in order to obtain the true perspective, the books should be read in the sequence given above. Otherwise some of the references in the later volumes to incidents narrated in the earlier may not be quite clear.

As to the personages concerned in the transmission of the messages : my mother passed into the higher life in 1909, aged sixty-three. Astriel was the Headmaster of a school in Warwick in mid-eighteenth century. Of Zabdiel's earth life I know little or nothing certain. Arnel gives some account of himself in the text.

---

[6] I have located a fifth volume and have published that as a Kindle ebook. All five volumes are now available as Kindle ebooks. GJC

Kathleen, who acted as amanuensis on the spirit side, lived in Anfield, Liverpool. She was a seamstress and died, at the age of twenty-eight, about three years before my daughter Ruby who is mentioned in the text and who passed over in 1896 at the age of fifteen months.

How The Messages Came

There is an opinion abroad that the clergy are very credulous beings. But our training in the exercise of the critical faculty places us among the most hard-to-convince when any new truth is in question. It took a quarter of a century to convince me—ten years that spirit communication was a fact, and fifteen that the fact was legitimate and good.

From the moment I had taken this decision, the answer began to appear. First my wife developed the power of automatic writing. Then through her I received requests that I would sit quietly, pencil in hand, and take down any thoughts which seemed to come into my mind projected there by some external personality and not consequent on the exercise of my own mentality. Reluctance lasted a long time, but at last I felt that friends were at hand who wished very earnestly to speak with me. They did not overrule or compel my will in any way—that would have settled the matter at once, so far as I was concerned-—but their wishes were made ever more plain.

I felt at last that I ought to give them an opportunity, for I was impressed with the feeling that the influence was a good one, so, at last, very doubtfully, I decided to sit in my cassock in the vestry after Evensong.

The first four or five messages wandered aimlessly from one subject to another But gradually the sentences began to take consecutive form, and at last I got some which were understandable. From that time, development kept pace with practice. The reader will find the result in the pages following.

G. Vale Owen.

Autumn, 1925.

Introduction

By Sir Arthur Conan Doyle

THE long battle is nearly won. The future may be chequered. It may hold many a setback and many a disappointment, but the end is sure.

It has always seemed certain to those who were in touch with truth, that if any inspired document of the new revelation could get really into the hands of the mass of the public, it would be sure by its innate beauty and reasonableness to sweep away every doubt and every prejudice.

Now world-wide publicity is being given to the very one of all others which one would have selected, the purest, the highest, the most complete, the most exalted in its source. Verily the hand of the Lord is here!

The narrative is before you and ready to speak for itself. Do not judge it merely by the opening, lofty as that may be, but mark the ever ascending beauty of the narrative, rising steadily until it reaches a level of sustained grandeur.

Do not carp about minute details, but judge it by the general impression. Do not be unduly humorous because it is new and strange.

Remember that there is no narrative upon Earth, not even the most sacred of all, which could not be turned to ridicule by the extraction of passages from their context and by over-accentuation of what is immaterial. The total effect upon your mind and soul is the only standard by which to judge the sweep and power of this revelation.

Why should God have sealed up the founts of inspiration two thousand years ago? What warrant have we anywhere for so unnatural a belief?

Is it not infinitely more reasonable that a living God should continue to show living force, and that fresh help and knowledge should be poured out from Him to meet the evolution and increased power of comprehension of a more receptive human nature, now purified by suffering.

All these marvels and wonders, these preternatural happenings during the last seventy years, so obvious and notorious that only shut eyes have failed to see them, are trivial in themselves, but are the signals which have called our material minds to attention, and have directed them towards those messages of which this particular script may be said to be the most complete example.

There are many others, varying in detail according to the sphere described or the opacity of the transmitter, for each tinges the light to greater or less extent as it passes through. Only with pure spirit will absolutely pure teaching be received, and yet this story of Heaven must, one would think, be as near to it as mortal conditions allow.

And is it subversive of old beliefs? A thousand times No. It broadens them, it defines them, it beautifies them, it fills in the empty voids which have bewildered us, but save to narrow pedants of the exact word who have lost touch with the spirit, it is infinitely reassuring and illuminating.

How many fleeting phrases of the old Scriptures now take visible shape and meaning?

Do we not begin to understand that "House with many mansions," and realize Paul's "House not made with hands," even as we catch some fleeting glance of that glory which the mind of man has not conceived, neither has his tongue spoken.

It all ceases to be a far-off elusive vision and it becomes real, solid, assured, a bright light ahead as we sail the dark waters of Time, adding a deeper joy to our hours of gladness and wiping away the tear of sorrow by assuring us that if we are only true to God's law and our own higher instincts there are no words to express the happiness which awaits us.

Those who mistake words for things will say that Mr. Vale Owen got all this from his subconscious self. Can they then explain why so many others have had the same experience, if in a less exalted degree?[7]

I have myself epitomized in two small volumes the general account of the other world, drawn from a great number of sources. It was done as independently of Mr. Vale Owen as his account was independent of mine.

---

[7] I have added a list of reading recommendations at the end which include books similar to this series, but also some I would consider more advanced. This is a very small selection of books on this topic. G.J.C.

Neither had possible access to the other. And yet as I read this far grander and more detailed conception I do not find one single point of importance in which I have erred.

How, then, is this agreement possible if the general scheme is not resting upon inspired truth?

The world needs some stronger driving force. It has been running on old inspiration as a train runs when the engine is removed. New impulse is needed. If religion had been a real compelling thing, then it would show itself in the greatest affairs of all—the affairs of nations, and the late war would have been impossible. What church is there which came well out of that supreme test? Is it not manifest that the things of the spirit need to be restated and to be recoupled with the things of life?

A new era is beginning. Those who have worked for it may be excused if they feel some sense of reverent satisfaction as they see the truths for which they laboured and testified gaining wider attention from the world.

It is not an occasion for self-assertion, for every man and woman who has been honoured by being allowed to work in such a cause is well aware that he or she is but in agent in the hands of unseen but very real, wise, and dominating forces. And yet one would not be human if one were not relieved when one sees fresh sources of strength, and realizes the all-precious ship is held more firmly than ever upon her course.

INTO THE LIGHT

The good God is, and God is good,
And when to us 'tis dimly seen
'Tis but the mists that come between
Like darkness round the Holy Rood,
Or Sinai Mount where they adored
The Rising Glory of the Lord.
He giveth life, so life is good,
As all is good that He has given.
Earth is the vestibule of Heaven;
And so He feeds with angel's food
Those in His likeness He has made,
That death may find us unafraid.
Death is no wraith, of visage pale,
Out of this darkened womb of Earth,
But waits attendant on our birth
To lead us gently through the Veil,
To realms of radiance, broad and free,
To Christ and immortality.

September, 1915.

Note. Subsequent to the reception of the portion of the script which is included in this volume, I received at three separate sittings the verses printed above. It was intimated to me, at that time, that the purpose for which this hymn was transmitted was that it should be regarded as a keynote to the messages received some years previously from my mother and her fellow-workers.

G. V. O.

Chapter 1

The Lowlands of Heaven

On the borderland—An initiation—"From strength to strength"—Sorrow and joy—Trees and flowers—The Chasm and the Bridge—"There is a great Gulf fixed"—The Cross of Light—"One Sinner who repenteth."

Tuesday, September 23, 1911

WHO is here?

Mother and other friends who have come to help. We are progressing very well, but are not able to give you all the words we would like to yet, as your mind is not so quiet and passive as we would wish.

Tell me something about your home and occupation.

Our occupation varies according to the needs of those to whom we minister. It is very various, but directed to the uplifting of those who are still in Earth life. For instance, it is we who suggested to Rose the creation of a band of people to come to her aid in case of her feeling any danger when she was in the room writing as we moved her hand, and that band is at present in charge of her case. Does she not feel their presence at times near her? She should do so, for they are ever near at call.

About our home. It is very bright and beautiful, and our companions from the higher spheres are continually coming to us to cheer us on our upward way.

A thought here came into my mind. Could they see these beings from the higher realms, or was it with them as with us? I may say that here and there throughout these records the reader will come upon passages which are quite obviously answers to my unspoken thoughts, usually beginning "Yes" or "No." This being understood, there will be no need for me to indicate them unless any particular instance seems to require it.

Yes, we can see them when they wish that we should do so, but that depends on the state of our advancement and their own power of service to us.

Now will you please describe your home, scenery, etc.?

Earth made perfect. But of course what you call a fourth dimension does exist here, in a way, and that hinders us in describing it adequately. We have hills and rivers and beautiful forests, and houses, too, and all the work of those who have come before us to make ready. We are at present at work, in our turn, building and ordering for those who must still for a little while continue their battle on Earth, and when they come they will find all things ready and the feast prepared.[8]

We will tell you of a scene which we witnessed not long ago. Yes, a scene in this land of ours. We were told that a ceremony was about to take place in a certain wide plain not far from our home, at which we might be present. It was the ceremony of initiation of one who had passed the gate of what we will call prejudice, that is, of prejudice against those who were not of his own particular way of learning, and who was about to go forth into a wider and fuller sphere of usefulness.

We went, as we were bidden, and found a great many people arriving from many quarters. Some came in… why do you hesitate? We are describing quite literally what we saw—chariots; call them otherwise, if you will. They were drawn by horses, and their drivers seemed to know just what to say to them, for they were not driven with reins like they are on Earth, but seemed to go where the drivers willed. Some came on foot and some through space by aerial flight. No, not wings, which are not necessary.

When they had all gathered, a circle was made, and one stepped out, the one who was to be initiated, and he wore a robe of orange colour, but bright, not like the colour as you know it; none of our colours are; but we have to speak to you in our old tongue. The one who had had him in his care then took him by the hand and placed him on a green knoll near the middle of the clear space, and prayed. And then a very beautiful thing occurred.

The sky seemed to intensify in colour—blue and gold mostly—and out of it descended a veil-like cloud, but which seemed to be made up of fine lace-work, and the figures dominating were birds and flowers—not white, but all golden and

---

[8] The reference to the feast should not be taken literally. In the Spirit Spheres spirits have no need of food, although they do enjoy water and are able to absorb the essence from fruit and nuts. But as they do not have digestive organs, they don't eat as we know it.

radiant. This slowly expanded and settled on the two, and then they seemed to become part of it, and it of them, and, as it slowly faded away, it left both more beautiful than before—permanently beautiful, for both had been advanced into a higher sphere of light.

Then we began to sing, and, although I could see no instrument, yet instrumental music blended with our singing and became one with it. It was very beautiful, and served both as a reward to those who had earned it and a spur to those who had still to tread the path they two had trodden. The music, as I found out later by inquiry, proceeded from a temple grove outside the circle, but indeed it did not seem to come from any one point. That is a faculty of music here. It seems very often to be part of the atmosphere.

Nor was the jewel lacking. When the cloud cleared, or dissolved, we saw it on the brow of the initiate, gold and red, and his guide, who had one already, wore his on his shoulder—left shoulder—and we noticed it had increased in size and brightness. I do not know how this happens, but have an idea, not definite enough to tell you, however, and it is difficult to explain what we ourselves understand. When the ceremony was over we all separated to our own work again. It was longer than I have described and had a very heartening effect on the rest of us.

Over the hill on the farther side of the plain to that where we stood I noticed a light grow up and it seemed to us a beautiful form in human shape. I do not think it was an appearance of our Lord, but some great Angel Master who came to give power, and to do His will. No doubt some there could see more clearly than I, because we are able to see, and also to understand, in proportion to our stage of advancement.

Now, my boy, just think for a moment. Is this from your mind or through it, as you say? When you sat down to write as you know, nothing was farther from your thoughts, for we had carefully refrained from impressing you, and yet you went off at once on the account as we influenced you. Is that not so?

Yes; I admit that frankly.

Quite right. And now we will leave—not you, for we are always with you in a way you do not understand—but we will leave this writing, with our prayer and blessing on you and yours. Good night and good-bye till to-morrow.

(Note.—When the whole series of messages was finished I reckoned up and found that the speed had been maintained at an average rate of twenty-four words a minute. On two occasions only had I any idea what subject was to be treated. That was when the message had obviously been left uncompleted. At other times I had fully expected a certain subject to be taken, but on taking up my pencil the stream of thought went off in an altogether different direction.)

Wednesday, September 24, 1913.

Suppose we were to ask you to look forward a little space and try to imagine the effect of our communications as viewed in relation to the ultimate outcome of your present state of mind. What then, think you, should have been the issue of events as we see them from our own sphere in the spirit world? It would be something like the effect of sunlight when it is projected into a sea-mist, which mist gradually vanishes away, and the scene it enveloped becomes clearer to the vision, and more beautiful than when dimly discerned through the enveloping mist.

So do we view your minds and, if the sun for awhile dazzles and perplexes rather than clarifies the sight, you know that the end is light, and the end of all that Light in whom there is no darkness at all. Yet light is not conducive to peace always, but, in its passage, often creates a series of vibrations which bring destruction to those species of living creatures which are not fashioned to survive in the light of the sun. Let them go, and, for yourself, go onward, and as you go your eyes will become used to the greater light, the greater beauty of the Love of God, the very intensity of which, blended as it is with infinite Wisdom, is perplexing to those who are not altogether of the light.

And now, dear son, listen while we tell you of one more scene which has gladdened us here in these regions of God's own light.

We were wandering a short time ago in a beautiful woodland place, and as we went we talked a little, but not more than a little because of the sense of music which seemed to absorb all else into its own holy silence. Then, standing in the pathway in front of us, whom should we see but an angel from a higher sphere. He stood and looked on us with a smile, but did not speak, and we became aware that he had a message for one of us especially. It was so, for, as we halted and stood in expectation, he came forward and, lifting the cloak he wore—amber it was in colour—he placed his arm and it round my shoulder and, laying his cheek on my hair—for he was much taller than I am—he said softly, "My child, I am sent to you from the Master whom you have learned to trust, and the way before you is seen by Him but not by you. You will be given strength for whatever you have to do; and you have been chosen for a mission which is new to you in your service here. You will be able, of course, to visit these your friends at will, but now you must leave them for a time and I will show you your new home and duties."

Then the others gathered round me and kissed me and held my hands in theirs. They were as glad as I—only that is not quite the word to use in my case, it is not peaceful enough. After awhile, when he had let us talk and wonder what his message meant, he came forward once more and this time took me by the hand and led me away.

We walked for a little time and then I felt my feet leave the ground and we went through the air. I was not afraid, for his strength was given to me. We passed over a high mountain range where many palaces were, and at last, after a fairly long journey, we descended in a city where I had not been before.

The light was not unkind, but my eyes were not used to such a degree of brightness. However, I soon made out that we were in a garden surrounding a large building, with steps up to it all along the front, at the top of which was a kind of terrace. The building seemed all of one piece of material of different hues—pink and blue and red and yellow—which shone like gold, but softly. Up these we went, and at the great doorway, without any door to it, we met a very beautiful lady, stately but not proud. She was the Angel of the House of Sorrow. You wonder at the word used in this connection. What it means is this: The sorrow is not of those who dwell there, but is the lot of those to whom they minister. The sorrowful ones are those on Earth, and it is the business of the residents in this House to send to them vibrations which have the effect of neutralizing the vibrations of sorrowful hearts on Earth.

You must understand that here we have to get at the bottom of things, and learn the cause of things, and that is a very deep study, only learned in gradual stages bit by bit. I therefore speak of the causes of things when I use the word "vibrations," as one you will understand best.

She received me very kindly and took me within, where she showed me over part of the place. It was quite unlike anything on Earth, so it is hard to describe. But I may say that the whole house seemed to vibrate with life, and to respond to our own will and vitality.

This, then, is my present and latest phase of service, and a very happy one it promises to be. But I have only just begun to understand the prayers which are brought to us there and registered, and the sighs of those in trouble we hear—or rather, they are also registered, and we see or feel them, as it were, and send out our own vibrations in answer. This in time becomes involuntary, but is a great effort at first, I find it so. But even the effort has a reflex blessing on those who work so.

There are many such places here, as I learn, all in touch with Earth, which at present would seem impossible to me except that, as the effects are also registered back again to us, I know the amount of comfort and help we send. I only am on duty for a short space at one time, and then go out and see the sights of this city and its neighbourhood. And very glorious it all is, even more beautiful than my old sphere, which I also revisit to see my friends. So you can imagine the talks we have when we do meet. That is almost as great a joy as the work itself. Peace in Jesus our Lord is the atmosphere all around us. And this is the land where there is no darkness and, when those mists are of the past, dear, you will come here, and I will show you all—until you are perhaps able to take me by the hand, as he did, and lead me to see the work in your own sphere. You think I am ambitious for you, dear lad. Well, so I am, and that is a mother's—shall I say weakness, or rather blessing?

Good-bye, dear. Your own heart at this moment is a witness that this is all real, for I can see it glowing happy and bright, and that is gladness also to me your mother, dear son. Good night, then, and God will keep you and yours in His peace.

Thursday, September 25, 1913.

What we want most to say to you tonight is to be

understood as a very imperfect attempt to tell you what is the meaning of that passage of which you have often thought where our Lord tells St. Peter that he is an adversary to Him. He, as you will remember, was on the way to the Holy City, and had been telling His Apostles that He would be killed there.

Now, what He evidently wished to impress on them was the fact that, although to men His mission might seem to have ended in failure, yet to eyes which were enabled to see as He would theirs might see, His end was only the beginning of a much more powerful and glorious development of the life-giving mission which He had undertaken on behalf of the Father and for the uplifting of the world.

Peter, by his attitude, showed that he did not understand this. Which is all plain and easy enough, so far, to understand. But what is usually lost sight of is the fact that the Christ was pursuing one straight line of progress, and that His death was but an incident in the way of His onward path, and that sorrow, as the world understands it, is not the antithesis of joy, but may be a part of it, because, if rightly used, it becomes the fulcrum on which the lever may rest which may lift a weight off the heart of the one who understands that all is part of God's plan for our good. It is only by knowing the real "value" of sorrow that we understand how limited it is in effect, so far as making us unhappy goes.

Now, He was about to inflict the heaviest sorrow He possibly could on the Apostles and, unless they understood this, they would be unable to use that sorrow to lift themselves above the turmoil of the world, and so, unable to do the work he had in hand for them to do. "Your sorrow shall be converted into joy," He told them, and so it came to pass, but not until they had learned the scientific value of sorrow—in a limited measure indeed, but in a measure nevertheless.

All this sounds very simple when it is written down thus, and no doubt it is simple, in a way, because all the fundamentals of God's economy are simple. But to us, and to me at the present time, it has an importance which may not be apparent to you. For the problem which is the chief study of the new House in which I spend so much of my time is this same subject, namely, the turning, or converting, of the vibrations of sorrow into the vibrations which produce joy in the human heart. It is a very beautiful study, but many perplexities enter into it because of the restrictions imposed on us by the sacredness of freewill. We may not overrule the will of any, but have so to work through their wills as to produce the desired effect and yet leave them free all the time, and so, deserving, in a way and in a measure at least, of the blessing received. I get tired sometimes, but that will pass away as I become stronger in the work. What is your question? I think you wish to ask one.

No, thank you, I have no particular question in mind.

Wasn't there something you wished to ask about something to do with the method by which we impress you?

I did think of asking you that this morning. But I had forgotten it. I suppose there is nothing much to explain, is there? I should call it mental impression.

Yes, that is correct, as far as it goes, but it does not go far. Mental impression is a phrase which covers up a great deal which is not understood. We impress you by means of these same vibrations, some of a different nature from others all directed on your will. But I see you are not much interested in that matter at the present moment. We will return to it, if you wish, at another time. I want to speak of those things which are of present interest to you.

Then tell me something more about that home of yours and your new work.

Very well, then, I will try to do so as well as I can.

It is beautifully appointed within and without. Within are baths and a music room and apparatus to aid us in registering our work. It is a very large place. I called it a house, but it is really a series of houses, each house allotted to a certain class of work, and progressive as a series. We pass from one to another as we learn all we can from any particular house. But it is all so wonderful that people would neither understand nor believe; so I would rather tell you of the simpler things.

The grounds are very extensive, and all have a kind of relation to the buildings, a kind of responsiveness. For instance, the trees are true trees and grow much as trees do on Earth, but they have a kind of responsiveness to the buildings, and different kinds of trees respond more to one house than to the others, and help the effect and the work for which that particular house was raised. So it is with the grouping of trees in the groves, and the bordering flower-beds of the paths, and the arrangement of the streams and falls which are found in different parts of the grounds. All these things have been thought out with marvelous wisdom, and the effect produced is very beautiful.

The same thing obtains on Earth, but the vibrations there are so heavy, comparatively, both those sent out and those which respond, that the effect is almost unseen. Nevertheless, it is so. For instance, you know that some people can plant flowers and trees more successfully than others, and that flowers will last longer in some houses—that is families—than others; cut flowers, we mean. All that is the same thing in grosser state.

Here these influences are more potent in action, and also the recipients more sensitive in perception. And that, by the way, is one of the things which help us to an accurate diagnosis of cases which are registered here for us to deal with.

The atmosphere also is naturally affected by vegetation and by buildings, for, let me repeat, those houses have not been raised merely mechanically, but are the outcome—growth, if you will—of the action of the will of those high in rank in these realms, and so of very powerful creative wills.

The atmosphere also has an effect on our clothing, and enters into the influence of our own personalities in its effect on texture and colour. So that while, if we were all of the same quality spiritually our clothing would be of the same tint and texture, by reason of the atmospheric influence, this is in fact modified by the degree in which our own characters differ one from another.

Also the tint of our robes changes according to the part of the grounds in which we happen to be. It is very interesting and instructive, and also very beautiful, to see them change as one turns down a side walk where different vegetation flourishes, or where the arrangement of the various species of plants is different.

The water also is very beautiful. You hear of water-nymphs and suchlike beings, in the Earth life. Well, I may tell you that here, at any rate, these things are true. For the whole place is pervaded and interpenetrated with life, and that means with living creatures. I had some idea of this in the sphere from which I have lately come, but here, as I grow accustomed to the strangeness and newness of it, I see it all much more plainly and begin to wonder what it will be a few spheres onward. For the wonder of this place seems to be about as much as any place could hold.

But there, let it rest. He Who enables us in one part of His beautiful Kingdom will enable us in another.

Which is a word for you, my dear son, and which I will, leave with you now, and my blessing.[9]

Friday, September 26, 1913

Our last instalment was given in answer to a request by one of our band that we should try to impress you in a rather deeper kind of way than heretofore, but we were only able to begin, as it were, and not to complete our explanation. If you wish it therefore, we will continue the subject now.

Thank you; yes.

Then you must, for a moment, try to think with us as from our side the Veil. Things, you must understand, take on a very

---

[9] Note by G.V.O.—While writing the first part of this message I could not see the drift of the argument, which seemed to me to be rather thin and muddled. On reading it over, however, I am by no means sure of my estimate.

Taking what is said of the vibrations of sorrow as merely a hint on "fundamentals," and applying to it some such reasoning as that by which the wave theory is applied to the radiation of light and heat, the result would be something like this: In dealing with that combination of vibrations which cause sorrow, the method is not so much that of substitution as of readjustment. By directing on the sorrowful soul other classes of vibrations those of sorrow are, some of them, neutralized; and others are modified and converted into vibrations the effect of which is joy or peace.

Viewed thus the above message does seem to hold some significance, and may perhaps throw light on the way in which troubles are actually dealt with in life. It certainly does seem to be part of the divine method, not that the outer aspect and circumstances of sorrow should be remedied (except in extremely rare cases), but that other elements should be infused which should have the effect of converting that sorrow into joy. This is merely a matter of everyday observation. To the unscientific mind this will probably seem to be drawing a very long bow. To others it may not seem so unreasonable to suggest that these "other vibrations" are really vibrations of other classes or "values."

The passage referred to is John xvi. 20: {Greek} η λυπη υμων εις χαραν γενησεται. —G.V.O.

different aspect here from what they did as viewed from the Earth plane, and an aspect, I fear, which to those still on Earth will, in many cases at least, wear a semblance of unreality and romance. And the least things here are fraught with so much wonder to those who are newly come over that until they have divested themselves of the habit of thinking in three dimensional terms, they are unable to progress very far. And that, believe me, is a matter of no little difficulty.

Now, the term "vibrations" is one which will have to serve, but it is far from adequate as understood of things material. For such vibrations as those of which we speak are not merely mechanical in movement and quality, but have an essence of vitality in themselves, and it is by that vitality that we are able to appropriate and use them. That is the connecting link between our wills and the outward manifestation in vibrations, for that is really all that these are. They are just phenomena of the deeper life which envelops us and all things. By them, as raw material, we are able to accomplish things, and build up things which have a durability which the term itself would seem to belie.

For instance, it is by this method that the bridge over the chasm[10] between the spheres of light and darkness is constructed, and that bridge is not all of one colour. On the farther side it is shrouded in darkness and, as it gradually emerges into, or towards, the region of light, it assumes an ever brighter hue and, where it lands on the heights where begin the brighter lands, it is of pink hue and glistens in the light enveloping it like some rare kind of silver, or alabaster rather.

Yes, of course there is a bridge over the chasm. Otherwise how would those who have fought their way upward through the gloom get over? True—and I had forgotten it—there are some who do proceed through the awful realm of darkness, and climb up the regions on this side the chasm. But these are few, and they are those obstinate ones who reject the help and guidance of those guardians of the way who are stationed on the farther side to show those who are qualified the way across.

Also, you must know, those guardians are only visible to those poor people, in proportion to the light that has been generated in their hearts; and so a certain amount of trust is

---

[10] See chapter 3.

needed if they would commit themselves to their keeping. This trust also is the outcome of a better mind by which they have become, in a measure, able to discern between light and darkness. Well, the complications of the human spirit are manifold and perplexing, and so let us get on to something easier of putting into words. I have called this a bridge, but—I ought to have referred you to the passage, "The light of the body is thine eye." Read that in this connection, and you will see that it bears on the case, not only of those on Earth but those here also. I have called this a bridge, but, as a matter of fact, it has little likeness to a bridge, on Earth.

For these regions are vast, and the bridge is more like a tract of country than anything else I can think of to call it to you. And remember I have only seen but a small part of these spheres, and so just tell you of that part which I know. Doubtless there are other chasms and bridges—probably numbers of them. Across the ridge, or bridge, then, those who seek the light make their journey, and that journey is but slow, and there are many rest-houses at which they stay, from time to time, on their progress across, and are handed on from one to another party of angel ministers, until the last stage lands them here on this side. Our work in the house, or colony, to which I now belong, is also directed to these progressive spirits, as well as to those on Earth. But that is a different department from mine at present. I have not yet got that far in my study.

For it is more difficult, because the influences around those in the darkness here are much more evil than the influences on Earth, where good influences are ever mingling with the bad. It is only when careless and wicked people get over here that they realize the awful task before them; and that is why so many of them remain for ages in a condition of hopelessness and despair.

When they are safely over the bridge they are welcomed by those on the slopes where grass and trees grow, and they are just stupefied with delight, in spite of the gradualness of their preparation. For they have not yet become used to love and its sweetness after their experience of the opposite down there.

I said this bridge landed on the heights; I speak comparatively. The landing place is highland as compared with those regions of darkness below. But, as a matter of fact, it is lowland, and the lowest land indeed, of the heavenly country.

You are thinking of the "great gulf," or chasm, "fixed," of the Parable.

That is all quite in accord with what I have written, and you have already had this explained to you elsewhere. Also the reason why these who come over do so instead of attaining this side by aerial travel, or "flight," as you would perhaps call it, is because they are not able to make the journey so on account of their weakness spiritually. If they were to attempt it they would only fall into the dark valley, and then lose their way.

I have not been far into those dark regions, but I have been a little way; and the misery I saw was quite enough to suffice for some time to come.

When I have progressed in my present work, and have for some time helped those poor souls from the vantage point of this house, I may be permitted, and probably shall be, to go farther among them. But that is not yet.

One thing more I may say—for it is time that you should cease. When they break away, and come to the other end of the bridge, I am told that the noises which are heard from behind them are horrible; and dull red flashes of fire are seen. How that is caused I am not able clearly to state, but we are told that both the yells and screeches and howls, and also the flashes, are made by those left behind who are enraged because of their powerlessness to recapture the fugitive, or to hold him as he is slipping away; for evil is ever powerless against good, be the good ever so small in amount. But I must not pursue this farther now, and what I am now saying is not what I have myself seen, but hearsay, that is, it is given to you at second-hand; but it is true, nevertheless.

Good night, then, dear son, and may the All Father shed His light and peace on you and yours...... In His light shall you see light; and the shining of that light is of the peaceful overbreaking dawn.

Saturday, September 27, 1913.

I asked my friends to try to impress me more vividly.

It is scarcely necessary that we should be careful to impress you more vividly than we have already done, for we have managed to get through the messages as we intended them, to help you to realize somewhat of our life, and conditions prevailing here. Only we would add that what should be clear to you is that—when we come here we are not in our own proper element, but that what to you is a natural environment is to us as a mist, and through it we have to work as best we can.

Are you able to see me as I sit here writing?

We do see you, but with other eyes than yours. Our eyes are not accustomed to the effect of light as you have it on Earth. Our light is of a different kind, a sort of interpenetrating element by which we are able to discern your inmost mind, and that is it to which we speak—to you yourself and not, of course, to your outward ears. So it is yourself we see, and not your material body, which is but an enveloping robe. When we touch you, therefore, you do not feel the touch physically but spiritually, and if you wish to apprehend our touch, you will have to keep this in mind and look deeper than the body and its mechanical brain.

You would wish to know something more of the way we work here and the conditions in which our life is spent, Not everyone who comes over here is able to understand that one of the elementary truths which it is necessary to assimilate in order to progress is that God is no more visibly present here than He is in the Earth life. They expect to see Him bodily, and are much disappointed when they are told that that is a quite mistaken idea of the way of His dealing with us. His life and beauty are quite apparent on Earth to those who can look deeper than the externals of nature. And so it is here, with this modification: that life here is more tangible, and easier to lay hold of and use by those who study its nature, and it pulsates all around us, and we, being in a more sensitive state, are more able to feel it than when we were in the Earth life. Still, having said this on the general conditions, it is true to add that, from time to time, manifestations of the Divine Presence are given us, when some particular purpose necessitates; and of one of these I will tell you now.

We were called to a tract of country where many people were to forgather, of different creeds and faiths and countries. When we arrived we found that a band of missionary spirits had returned from their period of duty in one of the regions bordering on the Earth sphere, where they had been working among souls just come over who did not realize that they had crossed the border-line between Earth and the spirit land. Many had been enlightened, and these had been brought to the place in order that they might join with us in a service of thanksgiving before going to their own proper homes. They were of various ages, for the old had not progressed yet in becoming youthful and vigorous again, and the young had not progressed to complete stature. They were all agape with happy expectation, and, as one company after another of their new companions in this life arrived, they scanned their faces, and the different coloured robes worn by the different orders and estates in wonder.

By and by we were all assembled, and then we heard a burst of music which seemed to invade us all and unify the whole great multitude into one great family. Then we saw a great cross of light appear. It seemed to lie on the slope of the great mountain which bordered the plain and, as we watched it, it began to break up into specks of bright light, and we gradually became aware that it was a large company of angels of a higher sphere who stood on the mountain in the form of a cross; and all about them was a golden glow, which we could feel at that distance as a warm breath of love.

Gradually they became more distinct to our vision as they emerged more perfectly into this, to them, lower environment, and then we saw, standing over the square where the arms of the cross joined the stem, a larger Being. We all seemed to know Him at once instinctively. It was a Manifestation of the Christ in what you have come to know as Presence Form.

He stood there silent and still for a long time, and then lifted His right hand on high, and we saw a column of light descend and rest upon it as He held it aloft. This column was a pathway, and on it we saw another company descending and, when they came to the uplifted hand, they paused and stood still with their hands folded on their breasts and heads bowed. Then slowly the hand moved out until it had swung round and down and the fingers pointed over the plain, and we saw the column stretch out towards us in mid-heaven until it bridged the space between the mountain and the plain, and the end of it rested over the multitude gathered there.

Along this column walked the company last become visible, and hovered above us. They spread out their hands then, and all slowly turned towards the mountain, and softly we heard their voices half speaking and half singing a hymn of devotion to Him Who stood there all so beautiful and so holy that at first we were awed into silence. But presently we also took up their words and sang, or chanted, with them; for that evidently was their purpose in coming to us. And as we sang there arose between us and the mountain a mist of bluish tint which had a very curious effect. It seemed to act like a telescopic lens, and brought the vision of Him nearer until we could see the expression on His face. It also acted similarly on the forms of those who stood just below Him. But we had no eyes for them only for His gracious face and form. I cannot describe the expression. It was a blend of things which words can only tell in small part. There were blended love and pity and joy and majesty, and I felt that life was a very sacred thing when it held Him and us in one bond. I think others felt something like this too, but we did not speak to one another, all our attention being taken up with the sight of Him.

Then slowly the mist melted into the atmosphere, and we saw the cross on the mountain and Him standing as before, only seen more dimly; and the angels who had come over to us had gone, and hovered above Him.

And then all gradually faded away. But the effect was a very definite sense of His Presence remaining and perpetual. Perhaps that was the object of the vision being given to the new-comers who, although they could not see so clearly as we could who had been here longer, yet would be able to see enough to encourage them and give them peace.

We lingered some time longer, and then quietly went our ways, not speaking much, because we were so impressed with what we had witnessed. And also, in all these Manifestations there is always so much to think out after. It is so glorious that one is not able, while it is taking place, to take in all the meaning. That has to be thought out gradually; and we talk it over, together, and each gives his impressions, and then we add them up, and find that a revelation has been given of something we did not understand before so well. In this instance what seemed to impress us most was the power He had of speaking to us in silence. He did not utter a word and yet we seemed to be hearing His voice speaking to us whenever He made a movement, and we understood quite well what the voice said, although it did not actually speak.

That is all I can tell you now, so, good-bye, dear son, and may you, as you will, see for yourself one day what our Lord has in store for them who love Him.

Monday, September 29, 1913.

The idea of viewing things from the standpoint of a higher sphere than yours is one which should be given due weight when you read what we have already written. Otherwise you will often be mystified at the seeming incongruity in the association of ideas as we have given them. To us it is perfectly natural to link together the coming of our Lord in Presence Form[11] and the other incident of the formation of that bridge which spans the great continent of the chasm. For what is there seen in the concrete—that is, of course, concrete to us here—is but a phenomenon of the same invisible power as that by which the Lord and His company of angel attendants bridged the gulf between the spheres in which we at present move and those from which these higher beings come.

You will understand that that manifestation was to us very much what materialization is to you. It was the linking up of two estates in the Kingdom of the Father by bridging the space by higher vibrations than those which we are able to use in these lower spheres. How it is done we can only surmise, but, having passed through from your Earth sphere into this, the connection between this and the next does not seem strange.

We would wish you could be further enlightened in regard to some of the wonders of our land, for then it would seem more natural to you, both during your sojourn on Earth, and also when you come over here it would be less unfamiliar to your mind. The former in that you would see that Earth is heaven in embryo, and heaven is but Earth cleansed and made perfect; and the latter for reasons quite obvious.

In order to help you in this matter, therefore, we will try to tell you of a system which we have here of separating and discerning between things that matter and those of lesser importance. Whenever we are perplexed about anything—and I speak just of our own immediate circle—we go up to the top of some building, or hill, or some high place where the surrounding country may be viewed from a distance. Then we state our difficulties, and when we have made the tale complete, we preserve silence for a time and endeavour to retreat into ourselves, as it were. After a time we begin to see and hear on a

[11] See the 1921 Preface.

higher plane than ours, and those things which matter, we find, are those which are shown to us, by sight and hearing, as persisting on that higher plane, in those higher spheres. But the things which do not matter so greatly we do not see nor hear, and thus we are able to separate the one class from the other.

It seems all right, dear, but could you give me a specific instance by way of example?

I think we can. We had a case of doubt to deal with, and scarcely knew how to act for the best. It was that of a woman who had been over here for rather a long time, and who did not seem able to progress much. She was not a bad sort of person, but seemed to be uncertain of herself and everybody around her. Her chief difficulty was about angels—whether they were all of light and goodness, or whether there were some of angelic estate and yet who were of the darkness. For some time we could not quite see why this should trouble her, as everything here seemed to be of love and brightness. But we found at last she had some relatives who had come over before her, and whom she had not seen, and could not find where they were. When we got at her real trouble we talked it over among ourselves, and then we went to the top of a hill and stated our wish to help her and asked to be shown the best way. A rather remarkable thing happened, as unexpected as helpful.

As we knelt there the whole summit of the hill seemed to become transparent and, as we were kneeling with bowed heads, we saw right through it, and a part of the regions below was brought out with distinctness. The scene we saw—and we all saw it, so there could be no delusion—was a dry and barren plain in semi-darkness and, standing leaning against a rock, was a man of large stature. Before him, kneeling on the ground, with face in hands, was another smaller form. It was that of a man, and he seemed to be pleading with the other, who stood with a look of doubt upon his face. Then at last, with a sudden impulse, he stooped down and caught the prostrate form to his breast, and strode with him over the plain towards that horizon where a faint light glimmered.

He went a long journey with that burden and, when they came to a place where the light was stronger, he set him down and pointed out the way to him; and we saw the smaller form thank him again and again, and then turn and run towards the light. We followed him with our eyes, and then saw that the other had directed him to the bridge, of which I have told you already—only that end of it which is on the other side of the chasm. Still we could not understand why this vision had been shown to us, and we continued to follow the man until he had reached the large building which stands at the entrance of the bridge—not to guard it, but to watch for those who come and who require refreshment and help.

We saw that the man had been sighted from the watchtower, for a flash of light signaled the fact to those below and to those on the next watchtower along the bridge.

And then the hill resumed its normal aspect again, and we saw no more.

We were more perplexed than ever now, and were descending the hill when our Chief Lady met us, and, in her company, one who seemed to be a high officer in some part of our spheres, but whom we had not met before. She said he had come to explain to us the instruction we had just received. The smaller man was the husband of the woman whom we were trying to help, and we must tell her to go to the bridge and she would be given a lodging there, where she could wait till her loved one arrived. The larger man whom we had seen was what the woman would call an angel of darkness, for he was one of the more powerful spirits in that dark land. But, as we had observed, he was capable of a good deed. Why then, we asked, was he still in the regions of darkness?

The officer smiled and said, "My dear friends, the Kingdom of God our Father is a very much more wonderful place than you seem to imagine. You never yet have met with a realm or sphere which was complete in itself, and independent and separate from all other spheres. Nor are there any such. That dark angel blends within his nature many spheres of knowledge and goodness and badness. He remains where he is first because of the badness remaining in him, and which unfits him for the regions of light. He remains also because, while he could progress if he would, yet he does not wish to do so at present, partly because of his obstinacy, and partly because he still hates the light, and thinks those who set out upon the awful uphill way fools because the pains and agonies are sharper then by reason of the contrast which they see between the light and the darkness.[12] So he remains; and there are multitudes such as he whom a kind of dull and numb despair prevents coming over. Also in his time of hatred and frenzy he is cruel. He had tortured and ill-treated this same man whom you saw with him from time to time, and that with the cruelty of a cowardly bully. But, as you saw, that wore itself out, and, when the man pleaded this last time, some soft chord in the heart of the other vibrated just a little, and, on the impulse, fearing a reversal of his intention, he liberated the victim who wished to make the journey, and pointed out to him the way, no doubt thinking in his heart that he was a fool and yet, perhaps, a wiser fool than he, after all."

This was new to us. We had not realized that there was any goodness in those dark regions before; but now we saw that it was but natural that there should be, or, if everyone were totally bad, no one would ever desire to come to us here.

But what bearing has all this on the discerning between the things which matter and those of lesser importance?

All that is of good is of God, and light and darkness, as applied to His children, are not, and cannot be, absolute. They are to be understood relatively. There are, as we now know, many "angels of darkness" who are in the darkness because of some twist in their natures, some obstinate trait which prevents the good in them having its effect. And these one day may pass us on the road of the ages, and become greater in the Kingdom of the Heavens than we who now are more blessed than they.

Good night, dear son. Think over what we have written. It has been a very wholesome lesson to us, and one which it were well if many in your present life could learn.

---

[12] This is a very curious issue which is also covered in other books. The moment a spirit decides to change and try to get out of the hells, they become more at the mercy of the other evil spirits. This is because it is a battle of wills, and as soon as a spirit has turned to God, it cannot any longer engage effectively in the battle. For this reason mostly, more advanced spirits come to their assistance to extricate them and it is their spiritual brightness that protects the more advanced spirits. G.J.C.

Chapter 2

Scenes that are Brighter

The Home of Music—"They stand, those Halls of Sion, all Jubilant with song, and bright with many an Angel"—The Halls of Colour—The heavenly life—A story with a moral—After death, realization and first experiences—A parting and a meeting—A children's school, progressive botany—A Manifestation—The child and the globe of light—All creation one—Creative thinking.

Tuesday, September 30, 1913

YOU would scarcely realize all that we feel when we come to Earth in this way, and commune with one still wending his way through the valley.

We feel that we are of those who are more than ordinarily privileged, for, once we are able to convince people how much lies to their hand that they might use for the uplifting of the race, there seems to be no bounds to the possibilities of good and enlightenment. Still, we are but able to do a little, and must rest content until others will co-operate with us, as you have done, fearlessly, knowing that no evil can come to those who love the Father, and serve Him in His Son, our Saviour Lord.

Now, in order to help those who still doubt us and our mission and message, let me say that we do not lightly leave our beautiful home to come down into the mists which surround the Earth sphere. We have a mission and a work in hand which someone must do, and there is joy in the doing of it.

A little time since—to speak in Earth phrase—we were sent into a region where the waters were collected into a large lake, or basin, and round the lake, at some distance from each other, were erected buildings in the form of large halls with towers. They were of varied architecture and design, and not all built of one material. Spacious gardens and woods surrounded them, some of them miles in extent, and full of beautiful fauna and flora, most of the species known on Earth, but also some which would be strange to you now, although I think that at least a proportion of them lived once on Earth. That is a detail. What I wish to explain to you is the purpose of these colonies.

They are for nothing else than the manufacture of music and musical instruments. Those who live there are engaged in the study of music and its combinations and effects, not only as to what you know as sound, but also in other connections. We visited several of the great houses and found bright and happy faces to welcome us and show us over the place; and also to explain what we were able to understand, and I frankly confess that was not much. Such as I personally did understand I will try to explain to you.

One house—or college, for they were more like colleges than manufactories, when I come to think of it—was devoted to the study of the best methods of conveying musical inspiration to those who had a talent for composition on Earth; and another house gave attention rather to those who were clever at playing music, and others to singing, and still others made a special study of ecclesiastical music, and others concert music, and others operatic composition, and so on.

The results of their studies are tabulated, and there their duty ends. These results are studied again by another class, who consider the best method of communicating them to composers of music generally, and then another body do the actual work of transmission through the Veil into the Earth sphere. Here are pointed out to them the objects of their endeavours, namely, those who are likely to prove most ready of response to their inspiration. These have been carefully selected by others who are trained in selection of such. All is in perfect order; from the colleges round the lake to the church or concert hall or opera house on Earth there is a chain of trained workers who are constantly active in giving to Earth some little gift of heavenly music. And that is how all your best music comes to you....

Yes, you are quite correct. Much of your music is not from us; and much is sullied in its passage. But that is not the fault of the workers from those spheres, but lies at the door of those on your side of the Veil, and those on this side who are of the gloomy regions and whom the character of the composer gives a foothold to tamper with that which comes from us here.[13]

---

[13] If one reads this very carefully, it is saying that just as we can get thought inputs from spirits of the light, so too can the evil spirits have

What were the towers for?

I was just going to explain that to you.

The lake is of vast extent, and the buildings at some little distance from it on all sides. But at certain times, previously arranged, the workers of some of these colleges, and now and again of all of them, send certain of their company to the tower top and, when all are assembled, then a concert, literally true to its name, is held. They all practise something they have previously agreed upon together. On one tower will be instrumentalists of one class, on another those of another class, and on the third vocalists; and on another, another class of vocalists; for there are many classes, not only four, as usually with you, but many toned voices. And other towers are devoted to other workers whose actual duties I could not understand.

From what I could make out, some of these were expert in harmonizing the whole, or part, of the volume of sound combined from the different towers.

But I want to get on to the description of the thing itself—the concert or festival, or whatever you like to call it. We were taken to an island in the midst of the lake, and there, in a beautiful scene of trees and grass and flowers and terraces and arbours of trees and little nooks and seats of stone or wood, we heard the festival.

First there came a chord, long and sustained, growing louder and louder, until it seemed to invade the whole landscape and waterscape and every leaf of every tree. It was the key given to the musicians on the various towers. It died into silence and all seemed very still. Then gradually, we heard the orchestra. It came from many towers, but we could not tell any single contribution apart. It was perfect harmony, and the balance of tone was exquisite.

Then the singers took up their part, It is of no use for me to try to describe this music of the heavenly spheres in Earth language, but I may perhaps be able to give you some idea of the effect.

Briefly, it made everything more lovely—not only beautiful,

---

input, and that the spiritual condition of the mortal is largely to blame for which of these is the more powerful or frequent. This is the Law of Attraction in action. G.J.C.

but lovely, too—for there is a difference in meaning of these two words as I use them here. All our faces took on a more lovely hue and expression, the trees became deeper in colour, and the atmosphere gradually grew into a vapour of tints like a rainbow. But the vapour did not obscure anything; it seemed to bring everything nearer together rather. The water reflected the rainbow tints, and our clothing also became intensified in colour.

Moreover, the animals and birds about us also responded. One white bird I remember especially. Her beautiful milky feathers gradually grew brighter and, when I saw her last, before she flew into a grove, she shone like gold burnished and glowing, like transparent light or fire. Then, as the mists slowly faded away, we all became, and everything became, normal once again. But the effect remained, and if I could give it a name, I should say it was "peace."

That, then, is one little experience which I had in the Home of Music. What we heard will be discussed again and again by meetings of experts, a little altered here, and a little there, and then some use will be made of it; perhaps at some great service of thanksgiving here, or some reception of spirits come over from the Earth life, or some other function. For music enters into so many phases of our life here, and, indeed, all seems music in these spheres of light—music and blended colour and beauty, all breathing love among all, and to Him Who loves us as we are not able to love. But His love draws us onward, and, as we go, is all about us, and we must inbreathe it, as we do the beauty of His presence. This we cannot choose but do, for He is All in All here, and love is a delight which only you will understand when you stand where we have stood, and heard what we have heard, and seen the beauty of His presence, breathing and shimmering all around and above and beneath, as we learned some little more of His love.

Be strong and live the valiant life, for the end is worth the cost, as we ourselves have proved.

Good night, dear lad, and remember that sometimes in your sleep we are able to waft some faint echo of such music as this into your spiritual environment, and it is not without its effect on the aspect worn in your mind by your next day's life and work.

Wednesday, October 1, 1913

What we said last evening relative to the Home of Music was but an outline sketch of all that we heard and saw; and we only went over part of the place. We are informed, however, that it is of much larger extent even than we thought at the time, and extends far away from the lake into the mountainous country outlying the plain in which the lake lies. In those mountains there are other colleges, all linked up with those we saw by means of a kind of wireless telephony, and a co-operative work is continually going on.

On our way back to our own home we turned aside to see another new thing. It was a plantation of very large trees in which was built another tower, not a single column, but a series of chambers and halls, with pinnacles and turrets and domes of manifold colours. These were all in the one building, which was very high and also spacious. We were shown within very courteously and kindly by one of the dwellers there, and the first thing that struck us was the curious aspect of the walls.

What had from the outside appeared opaque, from the inside were translucent, and, as we went from hall to hall, and chamber to chamber, we noticed that the light which filled each was slightly different in tint from the one which led to it—not of different colour, for the variance was not so marked as that, but just a slight degree deeper or lighter.

In most at least of the smaller compartments the light was of one definite and delicate hue, but every now and then, after passing through a more or less complete series of chambers, we came to a large hall, and in this hall were gathered all the component tints of the surrounding chambers. I am not quite sure whether I am exactly correct in saying that all the smaller laboratories only distilled one tint, but am telling you as nearly as I can remember. There was so much we saw that it is difficult to separate all into details; and it was my first visit. So I do not vouch for more than a true description of the general scheme.

One of these great halls was the Orange Hall, and in it were all the tints of that primary, from the faintest of light gold to the deepest of deep orange. Another was the Red Hall, where hues were ambient all about us, from the faintest rose-leaf pink to the deepest crimson of the rose or dahlia. Another, the Violet Hall, was radiant with hues ranging from the most delicate heliotrope, or amethyst, to the dark rich hue of the pansy. And now I must tell you that there were not only more but several more of these halls devoted to those tints which you do not know, but which you call the ultra-violet and the ultra-red, and most wonderful they are.

Now, these rays are not blended together in one hue, but each tint was distinct in its gradation, and yet A harmonized wonderfully and beautifully.

You are wondering to what purpose these buildings of crystal are put. They are for studying the effect of colours as applied to different departments of life, animal, vegetable and even mineral life, but the two former chiefly, together with clothing. For both the texture and the hue of our garments take their quality from the spiritual state and character of the wearer. Our environment is part of us, just as with you, and light is one component, and an important one, of our environment. Therefore it is very powerful in its application, under certain conditions, as we saw it in these halls.

I am told that the results of those studies are handed on to those who have charge of trees and other plant life on Earth and other planets. But there are other results which are too rare in nature for such application to the grosser environment of Earth and the other planets, so, of course, only a very small part of these studies is handed on in your direction.

I am sorry that I can tell you little more, partly because of these same limitations, and partly because it is rather scientific and out of my line. But this I may add, for I inquired while there. They do not gather the primary colours together in one hall in that colony. Why, I do not know. It may be, as some of my friends think, who understand these matters better than I do, that the force generated by such combination would collectively be too tremendous for that building and require a specially constructed one, and that, probably, away in some high mountain; as it is possible, they told me, that no vegetation would live within a long distance of such a place.

And they add that they doubt whether people of the degree we met could safely control such forces as would be so generated. They think it would require those of much higher state and skill. But away in another and higher sphere there may be, and probably is, a place where this is done, and that place in touch with the one we saw. Judging from the way things are ordered here, that much is almost certain.

We left the colony, or university, as it might be called, and when we were at some distance away on the plain where we could see the central dome above the trees, our guide, who had come with us to speed us on our way, told us to stop and see a little parting surprise which the Chief had promised to afford us. We watched and saw nothing, and, after a while, looked at our guide questioningly. He smiled, and we looked again.

Presently one of our party said, "What colour was that dome when we first paused here?" One said, "I believe it was red." But none could be sure. Anyway, it was then a golden tint, so we said we would watch it. Sure enough, presently it was green, and yet we had not seen it change, so gradually and evenly was the progress from one colour to the other made. This went on for some time, and it was extremely beautiful.

Then the dome disappeared utterly. Our guide told us it was still there in the same place, but the disappearance was one of the feats they had managed to accomplish by combining certain elements of light from the various halls. Then above the dome and the trees —the dome still being invisible—there appeared an enormous rose of pink, which slowly deepened into crimson, and all among its petals there were beautiful forms of children playing, and men and women standing or walking and talking together, handsome, beautiful and happy; and fawns and antelopes and birds, running or flitting or lying among the petals, whose shapes swelled like hills and mounds and landscapes. Over these swells ran children with the animals, playing very happily and prettily. And then it all slowly faded away, and all was blank. We were shown several of these displays as we stood there.

Another was a column of light which shot up vertically from where we knew the dome was, and stood erect in the heavens. It was of the purest white light, and so steady that it looked almost solid. Then came a ray from one of the halls obliquely and gently struck against the side of the column. Then came another from another hall, of a different colour—red, blue, green, violet, orange; light, middle and dark of all colours you know, and some which you do not know—and they all lodged against the white column about half way up.

Then we saw the oblique lines of light taking shape, and they slowly became each a highway with buildings, houses, castles, palaces, groves of trees, temples and all manner of such, all along the broadways. And up these ways came crowds of people, some on foot, some on horseback, and others driving in chariots. All on one shaft of light were of one colour, but manifold in hues. It was very lovely to see them. They approached the column and halted a little distance from it all round.

Then the top of the column opened out slowly, like a beautiful white lily, and the petals began to curl over, and lower, and ever lower, until they overspread the space between the people and the column. And then the base of the column began to do the same, until it formed a platform, circular in shape, between the different shafts of light, from the column to so far as the places on each causeway where the people halted.

Then they could move onward. But they mingled now, and their horses and conveyances, each retaining its own tint and colour, but mingling with the rest. And we became aware that what we were looking at was a great multitude of lovely and happy people, gathered as if for a feast or festival, in an enormous pavilion of varitinted light. For their hues were now reflected against and into the roof and the floor, or pavement, and most wonderful was the radiance of it all. Slowly they formed into groups, and then we noticed that the centre column was piped like a great organ, and we understood what to expect.

And it came very soon—a great burst of music, vocal and instrumental, a grand Gloria in excelsis to Him Who dwells in the light which is as darkness to His children, even as our darkness is as light when He sheds down on us a ray of His present power; for Omnipotent is the King Whose Light is life to all His children, and Whose glory is reflected in the light such as we are able to endure. Something like that they sang, and then all that, too, faded away. I expected they would retrace their steps along the causeways, but these were withdrawn, and apparently it was unnecessary.

Your time is up, dear lad, so we must stop regretfully, with our usual love to you, my dear one, and those who love you and us, as we love them. God be with you, Who is Light, and in Whom no darkness can find a place to rest.

Thursday, October 2, 1913

"Speak unto the children of Israel that they go forward."

That is the message we would impress on you now. Do not lag behind in the way, for light is shed along it which will show you the path, and, if you hold fast to your faith in the All Father and His dear Son our Lord, you need have no fear of any beside.

We write this on account of certain lingering doubts still about you. You feel our presence, we know, but our messages have taken on such a complexion as to seem too fairy-like to be real. Know, then, that no fairy story ever written can equal the wonder of these Heavenly Realms, or the beauties of them. Moreover, much of the description you read in fairy books of scenery and buildings is not altogether unlike many things we have seen here in this beautiful land.

Only a little yet have we been able to learn, but, from that little, we are convinced that nothing which can enter into the creative imagination of a man while in the Earth life can equal the glories which await his wondering intellect when he puts off the Earth body, with its limitations, and stands free in the light of the Heavenly Land.

Now, what we wish to try to tell you tonight is of a rather different order from our former messages, and has regard rather to the essential nature of things than to the phenomena of life as displayed for our instruction and joy.

If a man could take his stand here on some one of the high summits with which this landscape is crowned, he would behold some rather strange and unfamiliar sights. For instance, he would probably first observe that the air was clear, and that distance had a different aspect from that it wears on Earth. It would not seem far away in the same sense, for, if he wished to leave the summit on which he stood and go to some point near the horizon, or even beyond, he would do so by means of his will, and it would depend on the quality of that will, and his own nature, whether he went fast or slow; and also how far he could penetrate into the regions which lie beyond the various mountain ranges and whose—I suppose we shall have to use the word—atmosphere is of rarer quality than that in which his present lot is cast.

It is on account of this that we do not always see those messengers who come to us from the higher spheres. They are seen by some better than by others, and are only truly and definitely visible when they so condition their bodies as to emerge into visibility. Now, if we go too far in their direction—that is, in the direction of their home—we feel an exhaustion which disables us to penetrate farther, although some are able to go farther than others.

Again, standing on that summit, the observer would notice that the firmament was not exactly opaque to the vision, but rather in the nature of light, but light of a quality which intensifies as the distance from the surface of the landscape increases. And some are able to look farther into that light than others, and to see there beings and scenes enacting which others less developed are not able to see.

Also, he would see all around him dwellings and buildings of various kinds, some of which I have described. But those buildings would not be merely houses and work-places and colleges to him. From each structure he would read not its character so much as the character of those who built it and those who inhabit it. Permanent they are, but not of the same dull permanency as those of Earth. They can be developed and modified and adapted, in colour, shape and material, according as the need should require. They would not have to be pulled down, and then the material used in rebuilding. The material would be dealt with as the building stood. Time has no effect on our buildings. They do not crumble or decay. Their durability depends simply on the wills of their masters, and, so long as these will, the building stands, and then is altered as they will.

Another thing he would notice would be flights of birds coming from out the distance and going, with perfect precision, to some particular spot.

Now there are messenger birds trained on Earth, but not as these are trained. In the first place, as they are never killed or ill-used, they have no fear of us. These birds are one of the means we use to send messages from one colony to another. They are not really necessary, as we have other quicker and more business-like ways of communication. We use them more as pretty fancies, just as we use colours and ornaments for beauty's sake sometimes. These birds are always making flights, and are dear loving creatures. They seem to know what their business is, and love to do it.

There is a tale here that once one of these birds, in his eagerness to outstrip his fellows, overshot the others and projected himself into the Earth sphere. There he was seen by a clairvoyant man, who shot at him, and so astonished was the wanderer—not at the shooting, but at the sensation which he felt coming from the man's thoughts—that he realized that he was not in his right element somehow, and as soon as he realized that, he was back again here. What he had felt coming from the man's brain was the resolution and desire to kill, and, although he knew it was something uncanny, when he came to try to tell his other bird friends he was at a loss, because nothing of the kind is known here, and he could no more describe it than a bird from this realm could describe his life to one of the Earth sphere. So the other birds said that, as he had a tale to tell which he could not, he was to return and find the man and ask him what word he should use.

He did so, and the man, who was a farmer, said "Pigeon-pie" would best describe his idea. The bird returned and, as they could not translate the term into their language, or make any meaning of it, they passed a resolution to the effect that whoever should wish to visit Earth in future should place himself under guard until inquiries had been made as to whether he was in his own proper sphere or no.

And the moral of it all is this: Keep to your own appointed task which you will understand, and where you will be understood by those who are your fellow-servants in the work: and do not be too eager to shoot ahead before you are sure of your ground, or "atmosphere," or, thinking you are going forward, you may find yourself in a sphere which is below the one from which you started, and where the highest beings of that sphere are less progressed, in many ways, than the lowest of your own, and much less pleasant as company.

Well, that is a light story as a little interlude, and will serve to show you that we can laugh here, and be foolish wisely, and wise foolishly, on occasion, and that we are not grown-up much in some things since we left your Earth and came over here.

Good-bye, dear; keep up a merry heart.

Friday, October 3, 1913.

When you are in any doubt as to the reality of spirit communion think of the messages you have already received and you will find that in all we have written we have preserved a clear purpose throughout. It is that we may help you, and through you others also, to understand how natural all is here, if wonderful also. Sometimes, when we look back upon our Earth life, we feel a wistful longing to make the way of those still there a little clearer and brighter than was our own in our forward glances into the future life. We did not understand, and so we went on in uncertainty as to what really awaited us. Many, as we know, say that this is good, and yet, as we view things from our present vantage ground, we cannot agree that uncertainty is good when a definite goal is to be won. Certainty, on the other hand, gives decision and leads to courageous action, and if we may be given to implant in just a few of Earth's sojourners the certainty of life and brightness here for those who fight the good fight well, we shall be amply repaid for our journeys hither from our own bright home in light.

Now let us see if we can impress you to write a few words of the conditions which we found when we arrived here—the conditions, that is, of those who pass over here when they first arrive. They are not all of an equal degree of spiritual development, of course, and therefore require different treatment. Many, as you know, do not realize for some time the fact that they are what they would call dead, because they find themselves alive and with a body, and their previous vague notions of the after-death state are not, by any means, lightly thrown away.

The first thing to do, then, with such as those is to help them to realize the fact that they are no more in the Earth life, and, to do this, we employ many methods.

One is to ask them whether they remember some friend or relative, and, when they reply that they do so but that he is dead, we try to enable them to see this particular spirit, who, appearing alive, should convince the doubter that he is really passed over. This is not always the case, for the ingrained fallacies are obstinate, and so we try another method.

We take him to some scene on Earth with which he is familiar, and show him those whom he has left behind, and the difference in his state and theirs. If this should fail, then we bring to his recollection the last experiences he underwent before passing, and gradually lead up to the time when he fell asleep, and then try to connect up that moment with his awakening here.

All these endeavours often fail—more often than you

would imagine—for character is built up year by year, and the ideas which go to help in this building become very firmly imbedded in his character. Also we have to be very careful not to overtax him, or it would delay his enlightenment. Sometimes, however, in the case of those who are more enlightened, they realize immediately that they are passed into the spirit land, and then our work is easy.

We once were sent to a large town where we were to meet with other helpers at a hospital to receive the spirit of a woman who was coming over. These others had been watching by her during her illness, and were to hand her over to us to bring away. We found a number of friends round the bed in the ward, and they all wore long dismal faces, as if some dire disaster was about to happen to their sick friend. It seemed so strange, for she was a good woman, and was about to be ushered into the light out of a life of toil and sorrow and, lately, of much bodily suffering.

She fell asleep, and the cord of life was severed by our watching friends, and then, softly, they awoke her, and she looked up and smiled very sweetly at the kind face of one who leaned over her. She lay there perfectly happy and content until she began to wonder why these strange faces were around her in place of the nurses and friends she had last seen. She inquired where she was, and, when she was told, a look of wonder and of yearning came over her face, and she asked to be allowed to see the friends she had left.

This was granted her, and she looked on them through the Veil and shook her head sadly. "If only they could know," she said, "how free from pain I am now, and comfortable. Can you not tell them?" We tried to do so, but only one of them heard, I think, and he only imperfectly, and soon put it away as a fancy.

We took her from that scene, and, after she had somewhat gained strength, to a children's school, where her little boy was, and, when she saw him, her joy was too great for words. He had passed over some few years before, and had been placed in this school where he had lived ever since. Then the child became instructor to his mother, and this sight was a pretty one to see. He led her about the school and the grounds and showed her the different places, and his schoolmates, and, all the while, his face beamed with delight; and so did the mother's.

We left her awhile, and then, when we returned, we found

those two sitting in an arbour, and she was telling him about those she had left behind, and he was telling her of those who had come on before, and whom he had met, and of his life in the school, and it was as much as we could do to tear her away, with a promise that she should return soon and often to her boy.

That is one of the better cases, and there are many such, but others are otherwise.

Now, while we waited for the mother who was talking with her son, we wandered over the grounds and looked at the various appliances for teaching children. One especially engaged my attention. It was a large globe of glass, about six or seven feet in diameter. It stood at the crossing of two paths, and reflected them. But as you looked into the globe you could see not only the flowers and trees and plants which grew there, but also the different orders from which they had been derived in time past. It was very much like a lesson in progressive botany, such as might be given on Earth and deduced from the fossil plants of geology. But here we saw the same plants alive and growing, and all the species of them from the original parent down to the present representative of the same family.

We learned that the task set for the children was: to consider this progression up to this particular plant or tree or flower actually growing in that garden and reflected in the globe, and then to try to construct in their minds the further and future development of that same species. This is excellent training for their mental faculties, but the results are usually amusing. It is the same study which full-grown students are also at work upon in other departments here, and is put by them to a practical end. One of them thought it would be a useful method to help the children to use their own minds, and so constructed the ball for their especial use. When they have thought out their conclusion, they have to make a model of the plant as it will appear after another period of evolution, and fearful and wonderful some of those models are, and as impossible as they are strange.

Well, I must not keep you longer, so we will continue when you are able to write again. God bless you and yours. Good night.

Monday, October 6, 1913.

Well, dear, you have had a very happy Harvest

Thanksgiving, and we were with you although you did not see us, and were too busy to think about us very much. We love to come and join with our fellow-worshippers still incarnate, and also to give what we are able to help in their worship. It may surprise you to know that here in these Realms of Light, we too, from time to time, hold such services as yours, and join in thanking our Father for harvest plenty. We do this by way of supplementing the thanksgiving of our brethren on Earth, and also for our own uplifting. We have here no such harvests as yours, but still we have services of thanksgiving for other blessings which are to us what harvest is to you.

For instance, we thank Him for the beauty all around us and all the glories of light and love which sustain us in vigour for our work and progress, and have services of thanksgiving for such blessings as these. At such times we usually are given some Manifestation from the Higher Spheres, one of which I will tell you about now.

We were holding our Eucharist in a valley, where two lofty hills stood some little distance apart, one on each side, but at one end of the vale. We had offered up our praises and worship, and stood with heads bowed down awaiting, in that silent peace, which always fills us at such times, for the word of Benediction from him who had been the chief minister. He stood a little way up the hillside, but he did not speak, and we wondered why.

After awhile we all slowly raised our heads, as if by one consent and impelled thereto by some inner voice, and we saw that the hill on which he stood was covered with a golden light which seemed to rest upon it like a veil. This slowly drew together and concentrated around the form of the Priest, who stood as if oblivious of anything about him. Then he seemed to come to himself again, and, stepping out of the cloud, he advanced towards us and told us that we were to wait awhile until we were able to see into the higher sphere from which certain angels of that sphere had descended and were present. So we waited, well content; for we have learned that when such an injunction is given it will presently be justified.

The cloud then lifted and spread out over the valley, farther and farther, until it covered the whole sky above us, and then it gradually descended and enveloped us, and we were in a sea of light far brighter than the light of our own sphere, but yet not dazzling to our eyes, but soft and mellow. By and by we were able to see by means of it, and then we saw the vision prepared for us.

The two high hills at the end of the valley glowed with fire, and each was the side, or arm, of a Throne, and about that Throne all colours of the rainbow played, much like that scene of which you read in the Book of Isaiah and of the Revelation. But we did not see the One Who sat on the Throne, at least not in bodily form. What we did see was a Manifestation of Him as to His Fatherhood. On the terrace, which was instead of the seat of the Throne, we saw a great company of Angels, and they were all bending in worship and love over a cradle. In the cradle we saw a child who smiled at them, and at length raised his hands towards the open space above him, where a light seemed to stream down from above.

Then into his arms there descended a golden globe, and he stood up and held it on his left hand. It seemed alive with the light of life and sparkled and glowed and became brighter and brighter until we scarcely noticed anything else but that ball itself and the child who held it, and whose body seemed to be irradiated through and through by its living light. Then he took it in his two hands and opened it in two halves, and held it aloft, turning the open circles towards us. One was filled with a pink radiance, and the other with blue. In the latter we saw the heavenly realms set in concentric circles, and each circle full of glorious and beautiful beings of those realms. But the outer circles were not so bright as the inner ones, and yet we could see the inhabitants more plainly because they were more nearly of our own estate than those others. As the innermost circles were neared, the light became too intense to see clearly what they held. But the very outermost circle we recognized as that of our own order.

The other bowl of pink light was different. There were no circles apparent in it. But yet, in perfect order, we beheld all the different species of animal and vegetable life as they are on the planets, including Earth. But we saw them not as they are with you, but in perfection, from man to the lowest form of sea-animal, and from the largest tree and most luscious fruit to the tiniest weed which grows. When we had viewed these awhile the child gently brought the two halves together, the glorious Heavens and the perfect Material Creation, and, when he had joined them, we could see no mark of the joining, nor tell which was one half and which the other.

But as we looked on the reunited ball, we saw that it was enlarging, and, at last, it slowly floated up from the hand of the child and rose into the space above him, and stood there poised, a beautiful ball of light. Then there gradually emerged into view, standing on the great sphere, the figure of the Christ, Who in His left arm held a cross, the base of which rested on the globe and the top was some little space above His shoulder. In His right hand He held the child, on whose forehead we now noticed a single circle of gold worn, as a fillet on his head, and over his heart a jewel like a great ruby. Then the globe began slowly to ascend into the heaven above, and the higher it went the smaller it grew to our sight, until it melted into the distance over the space between the two hills.

Then we were in our normal state again, and all sat down to wonder at what we had seen, and the meaning of it. But although some seemed to have some glimmerings as to the meaning of it, nobody was very illuminative. Then we thought of our minister, who had first received the baptism of the cloud, and, as it seemed to us, in a more intense degree than the rest of us. We found him sitting there by himself on a rock, with a quiet smile on his face, as if he knew we should come to him at last, and was waiting till we remembered him. He bade us sit down again, and, still sitting on the rock where he could be seen by all, he told us of the Vision.

It had been explained to him as to its more obvious meanings, and these he was able to hand on to us, leaving us to think it over and work out the higher and inner teaching for ourselves, each according to his own phase of mind. This is what is usually done, I find, when teaching is given to us by such means as this.

The pink hemisphere represented the Creation which was inferior to our Sphere, and the blue one our own and that superior to us. But these were not two Creations, but one; and there was no break between these two hemispheres or any of their sub departments. The child was the embodiment of the beginning, progress and end, which has no ending—our onward way. The ruby stood for sacrifice, and the crown for achievement, and the ascension of the globe and the Christ and the child led our aspirations into those realms which are at present beyond our attainment.

But of course, there is much more than this mere outline in it, and we are, as I said, left to work it out for ourselves. This, according to our custom, we shall do, and, at future gatherings, give our conclusions from time to time, and discuss them.

Thank you. May I now ask you a question which I have been requested to put to you?

No need to put it into words. We can see it in your mind, and knew it before you wrote.[14] The dove which Miss E. saw above the altar of your church was a manifestation, in presence form, such as that I have just related. It was for your invisible congregation, and symbolized, in a way they would readily understand, the gentleness of the presences about the altar, that they were there indeed in love, and ready to help those who were willing to receive their help, and, in token of their gentleness, a dove was seen hovering near them and unafraid; a state of mind which those who are not progressed are not always able to maintain in the presence of those from the higher realms whose bright holiness sometimes, in the minds of those who are not able to judge proportionately, by reason of their still lingering imperfections, eclipse their other virtues and make the poor doubting ones afraid.

Wednesday, October 8, 1913.

Because of certain matters which are of importance to those who would understand our meaning in its inner sense, we have decided to endeavour tonight to give you some instruction which will be of help and guidance when dealing with those things which lie beneath the surface of things, and which are usually not taken into account by the ordinary mind.

One of these is the aspect which thoughts wear when projected from your sphere into ours.

Thoughts which are good appear with a luminance which is absent from those of a less holy kind. This luminance appears to

---

[14] A member of the congregation of All Hallows, Orford, had told me a few days previously that she had seen clairvoyantly a dove hovering over the altar during the celebration of the Holy Communion—G.V.O.

issue from the form of the thinker, and, by means of its manifold rays of divided colours, we are able to come at some knowledge as to his spiritual state, not alone as to whether his state is of the light or of the darkness, and of what degree in light, but also of the points in which he excels or comes short in any direction. It is by this that we are able to allot to him the guardians who will best be able to help him in the fostering of that which is good in him, and in the cleansing away of that which is not good or desirable. By means of a kind of prismatic system we divide up his character, and so reach our conclusions, which are based on the result.

In this life such a method is unnecessary, for it is a matter concerning the spiritual body, and here, of course, that body is patent to all, and, being a perfect index of the spirit, shows forth his characteristics. Only I may say that the colours of which I have spoken are here communicated, in a degree, to our clothing, and those which are dominant over the others serve to classify us into our various spheres and grades. But thoughts which are the effect of spirit action, are seen in the effect they, in their turn, produce on the environment of the thinker, and not only are seen, but felt, or sensed, by us in a more accurate and intense way than with you.

Following on this line of reasoning, you will naturally see that when we think anything very intensely our wills are able to produce an outward manifestation which is really objective to those who behold it. Thus are many beautiful effects produced.

Can you give me a particular instance, by way of illustration?

Yes; it will help you to see what we mean.

A company of my friends and myself, who were being instructed in this knowledge, met together in order to see how far we had progressed, and resolved on an experiment to that end. We selected a glade in the midst of a beautiful wood, and, as a test, we resolved all to will one particular thing, and see if we were successful. What we selected was the producing of a phenomenon in the open space which should be so solid and permanent as to allow of us examining it after-wards. And that was to be a statue of an animal something like an elephant, but rather different; an animal which we have here, but which has ceased to inhabit your Earth.

We all sat round the open space and concentrated our wills on the object to be produced. Very quickly it appeared and stood there before us. We were much surprised at the quickness of the result. But, from our point of view, there were two defects. It was much too large; for we had failed to regulate the combination of our wills in due proportion. And it was much more like a live animal than a statue, for many had thought in their minds of the live animal itself, and also of its colouring, and so the result was a mixture between stone and flesh. Also many points were disproportionate—the head too large and the body too small, and so on, showing that more power had been concentrated on some parts than on others. It is thus we learn our imperfections, and how to remedy them, in all our studies. We experiment, and then examine the result, and try again. We did so now.

Taking our minds off the statue so produced, and talking together, it gradually faded away. And then we were fresh and ready for our next trial. We decided not to select the same model as before, or our minds would probably run into more or less the same grooves. So we, this time, chose a tree with fruit on it—something like an orange tree, but not quite the same.

We were more successful this time. The chief points of failure were that some of the fruit was ripe and some unripe. And the leaves were not correct in colour, nor the branches rightly proportioned. And so we tried one thing after another, and found ourselves a little more successful each time. You can imagine somewhat of the joy of such schooling as this, and the laughter and happy humour which result from our mistakes. Those among you who think that in this life we never make jokes, and never even laugh, will have to revise their ideas some day or they will find us strange company—or perhaps we shall find them so. But they soon learn what the love of this land is, where we can be perfectly natural and unrestrained, and indeed are compelled to be so if we wish to be accepted into respectable company, as you would phrase it. I fear the obverse is rather true on Earth, is it not? Ah well, live and learn, and those who live in this life—and not merely exist, or worse—learn very quickly. And the more we learn, the more we marvel at the forces at our command.

Astriel,[15] who came yesterday—is he here now!

---

[15] Astriel's messages were given on various dates which, however, were not consecutive. Why they were given in this way is not apparent. The effect, however, was to cut into the communications given by Mr. Vale

Not tonight. But he will, no doubt, come again, as you wish it.

Thank you. But I hope you will come and write too.

Oh yes, we will do so, for it is practice both for you and for us also, for, in thus impressing you, we are learning to use our wills and powers in a similar way to that I have been describing. Do you not see the image of the things we are telling you in your mind?

Yes, very vividly sometimes; but I had not thought of it in that way.

Ah well, my boy, you see now, do you not, that we had an object in writing what we have above? All the time you were thinking it was rather thin (and perhaps it was—we do not say to the contrary), and you were wondering whither it all was tending, and, in your mind, you were just a very wee bit disgusted. Now, were you not, dear? Well, we were smiling all the time; and now you understand that you were interpreting our thoughts, more or less, as we sent them forth, and the object we had was to explain to you how those scenes appeared before you so vivid and so real, as you described them.

Good-bye, dear lad, and God bless you and your dear ones now and always.

Owen's mother in such a way as rather to break the continuity of her messages as well as to destroy the sequence of those of Astriel himself. I have deemed it advisable, therefore, to collect them into a separate chapter. See chapter six.—H.W.E.

Chapter 3

From Darkness into Light

At the Home of Arnol—A lesson in wisdom—Evolution, inverted and progressive—The science of creation—The entity the "Name"— Chasm and the Bridge—"Send out Thy light" to "lead me"— From darkness into light—Angels can suffer—Angelic ministry.

Friday, October 10, 1913

WERE we to impress you to write on matters which to us are of everyday concern, you would perhaps be able to compare them with your own daily life, and you would see then that we and you are both at school, and that the school is a very large one, with many classes, and many instructors,—but with one scheme running throughout the course of instruction, and that scheme a unity of progress from the simple to the complex, and that complexity does not mean perplexity, for, as we learn more of the wisdom of the Divine Author of all, we see how beautifully composite is the realm in which He exerts His Loving Will to the end we may, by our very joy of knowledge, give homage to the Glory of Him Who holds all things in the hollow of His Hand.

And so, dear lad, we will once again take up our theme, and tell you of our doings here in these bright realms, and of how the Father's love encompasses us all around as a radiant cloud in which all things appear to us more plainly—as we progress in humility and in love.

One of those things which matter here is that due proportion be meted out between wisdom and love. These are not contrary the one from the other, but are two great phases of one great principle. For love is to wisdom as the tree is to the leaves, and if love actuate and wisdom breathe, then the fruit is healthy and sound. By way of illustrating this we will give you a concrete instance of how we are taught to consider duly both love and wisdom in our dealings with ourselves and others to whom we are permitted to minister.

We were given a task to perform a short time ago in which

a party of us, to the number of five, were to go to a colony in a rather distant part of this land, and inquire of them by what means could best be given help to those on Earth who were in doubt and perplexity as to God's Love. For we were often hampered by our lack of experience in dealing with such cases, and these cases, as you know, are many.

The Principal of the College was a man who in Earth life had been a statesman of no little ability, but his fame was not so great, and it was only when he came over here that he found play for his powers, and understood that the Earth is not the only field in which Earth's training may be put to use and effect in the Kingdom of God.

We stated to him the object of our mission, and he was very courteous and kind, for all his high office. I suppose you would call him a great angel, and indeed, if he could come to Earth and assume visibility, his brightness would be somewhat awe-inspiring. He is very beautiful, both of form and countenance; radiant and beaming and glowing would perhaps describe him best. He listened and encouraged us, now and then, with a quiet word, to state our difficulties, and we forgot that he was so high in estate, and talked without fear or restraint. And then he said, "Well, my dear pupils—for so you are good enough to become for a little time—what you have told me is very interesting, and also very general in the work in which you are now engaged. Now, if I were to solve your perplexities you would go back to your work with light hearts, but you would probably find that the solution, when it came to work out, would not be without many flaws in the working, for just those points which are most necessary to remember are those little things which can best be learned by experience; and experience is the only thing which can show you how great these little things are. Come, therefore, with me, and I will teach you what is necessary for you to learn in a better way."

So we went with him, and he led us into the grounds which surrounded his house, and there we found there were gardeners at work tending the flowers and fruit trees, and doing the general work of a garden. He took us some distance along the walks, winding here and there, and through plantations of trees and shrubs, where birds were singing and small pretty furry animals played here and there. At length we came to a stream and by it stood a stone arbour, which reminded me of a miniature temple of

Egypt, and led us within. Then we sat on a seat under a network of flowering plants of different colours, and he sat on another bench at right angles to us.

Drawn on the floor, in indented lines, was a plan, and he pointed to it and said, "Now, this is a plan of my house and these grounds through which I have led you. Here is marked this little place in which we sit. We have come, as you will see, a considerable distance from the gate where I met you, and you were all talking so much of the pretty things you saw as you came that not one of you gave heed to the direction in which you came. It will be good practice, therefore, and not altogether lacking in pleasure, for you to find your way back again to me, and, when you arrive, I shall perhaps be able to give you some help by way of instruction on the difficulties you have stated to me."

With that he left us, and we all looked at one another, and then burst out laughing at ourselves for being so foolish as not to guess his object in leading us to this place by so circuitous a route. We then examined the plan again and again, but it was all lines and triangles and squares and circles, and we could make little of it at first.

Gradually, however, we began to understand. It was a map of the estate, and the arbour was in the centre, or nearly so, but the entrance was not shown, and, as there were four paths leading up to it, we did not know which to take to get back again. We, however reasoned that it did not matter much, for all seemed to lead to the outer circle; because there were so many paths between us and that, which crossed and recrossed each other. I must not tell you of all our endeavours to solve the problem, as it would take much too long.

At last I had a thought which I considered, and then, thinking it might perhaps help, told the others. They said it was the very thing they had been waiting for, and would very likely prove the key to the riddle. It was nothing more wonderful than just to go out and take whatever path led in the most direct line onwards from any we were forced to leave. That is awkward —what I mean is this: to go by those paths which would lead us in the straightest line from the arbour in any direction whatever. Then, when we had reached the boundary, which we saw by the plan was a perfect circle, we could skirt that and must inevitably reach the gate sooner or later.

So we set off, and a long and very pleasant journey it was, and not without adventure, for the place was extensive, with hills and valleys and woods and streams, and all so beautiful that we had to keep our object very firmly before our minds or we should have forgotten to choose the correct path when we came to two ways.

We reached the outermost boundary, however, although we did not, I think, take quite the best and most direct route. This boundary, I may say in passing, was composed of a wide stretch of grassland, and we saw, by the shape of its border, that it was circular, although we could not see much of it. So we turned to the left and then, as we went on, the bend of the circular estate seemed endless. Still we followed it and eventually came to the gate where first we had met our instructor.

He greeted us encouragingly, and we went up on to a terrace before the house, and then told him all our adventures—much more than I have narrated to you—and he listened as before, and then said, "Well, you have not done so badly, for you have gained your object, you have returned to the gate. And now let me tell you the lesson you have learned.

"First of all, the thing is to make sure of the direction you wish to go; and then the next thing is to take, not the path which seems shortest, but the one which seems surest to lead you right in the end. That path will not always be the quickest, and may lead you to the borderland where infinity shades off from the realm you know. Still, beyond the border line you are the better able to see both the extent and also the limitation of the estate you are negotiating, and it is only a matter of steadfastness and patience, and the goal you desire is quite sure to be won.

"Also, from just beyond the boundary between the local and the infinite, you are able to see that, although it contains within itself paths winding and many, and valleys and groves from which you cannot see very far away, yet that, viewed as a whole, it is perfectly symmetrical—a true circle in fact, which, for all the seeming maze and medley within, yet, as a circle, contains within itself a perfect geometrical entity, simple in itself, considered as a unit from the larger, wider point of view; perplexing when passing through its paths inside the boundary line.

"Also, you noted that, as you followed that curve on its outer side, you were able only to see a little portion of it at one time. Still, knowing that, from its shape, it would lead to the place you sought, you were content to follow on in faith based on reasoned conclusions, and, true enough, here you are and prove by your presence that your reasoning was, at least in the main, sound.

"Now, I could pursue this subject considerably further, but I will hand you over now to some of my friends who are with me here and help me in the work, and they will show you more of our home and its surroundings, and, if you wish, will be glad to accompany you farther afield, for there is much of interest to show you. Also you will be able to talk over with them the lessons I have been happy enough to be able to give you, and among you you will, no doubt, have something more to tell and to ask me when we meet a little later."

So he bade us good-bye, and a band of happy people came from the house and led us within. But, as the time is up for you to go to other duties, we must cease now, with our love and assurance to you of our delight in coming thus to commune with you, if only for this little while.

God bless you, dear lad, and all our loved ones. Mother and friends.

Saturday, October 11, 1913.

We were able to give you only a very brief account last evening of our visit to the home of our instructor on account of the shortness of time. We will now continue, and relate some of our experiences in that region. It is a region where there are many such institutions, and they are mostly devoted to the study of the best way of helping those on Earth who are in doubt and perplexity as to the problems which stretch out into the realms beyond. You will be able, by meditation, to amplify our own instruction if you view the place and our experience there in the light of a parable. So we pass on to other scenes, and will describe them as well as we can.

Our guides led us to a place outside the boundary of the estate of which we have already spoken, and we found that the grass-land was very extensive. It is one of those plains of Heaven where manifestations from the higher Heavens are sometimes given. The call goes forth and vast multitudes assemble, and then some of the glories of the higher spheres are manifested, as well as is possible in these lower realms.

We passed over this tract until we at length began to ascend, and presently found ourselves on a tableland, where there were several buildings scattered about, some larger than others. In the centre was a large structure, and this we entered and found ourselves in a large and spacious hall, the only compartment in the place. It was circular in shape, and round the walls were carvings of a curious kind. We examined them and found that they were representations of the heavenly bodies; and one was the Earth. But they were not fixed, but turned on pivots, half in and half out of the wall. There were also models of animals and trees and human beings, but they were all movable, and mostly stood on pedestals in niches or alcoves. We inquired the meaning and were told that this was a purely scientific institution.

We were taken up to a balcony on one side of the circular space. It projected somewhat, and so we could see the whole at once. Then we were told that a small demonstration would be made for our benefit in order that we might get some idea of the use to which these things were put.

We sat there waiting, and at length a blue mist began to fill the central space. Then a ray of light swept round the hall and rested on the globe which represented the Earth. As it hovered about it the sphere appeared to absorb the ray and became luminous, and after a time, the ray being withdrawn, we saw the Earth globe was shining as from within. Then another ray was sent on to it of a deeper and different kind, and the globe slowly left the pedestal, or pivot, or whatever it rested on, and began to float out from the wall.

As it approached the centre of the space it entered the blue mist and immediately on contact began to enlarge until it became a great sphere glowing with its own light and floating in the blue space. It was exceedingly beautiful. Slowly, very slowly, it revolved on its axis, evidently in the same way the Earth does, and we were able to see the oceans and continents. These were flat patterns, like those on the terrestrial globes used on Earth. But as it revolved they began to assume a different aspect.

The mountains and hills began to stand out, and the waters to sway and ripple; and presently we saw minute models of the cities, and even details of the buildings. And still more detailed grew the model of Earth, till we could see the people themselves, first the crowds and at last the individuals. This will be hard for you to understand, that on a globe of some, perhaps, eighty to a hundred feet in diameter we were able to see individual men and animals. But that is part of the science of this institution—the enabling of these details being seen individually.

Still more distinct grew these wonderful scenes, and, as the globe revolved, we saw men hurrying about the cities and working in the fields. We saw the wide spaces of prairie and desert and forest and the animals roaming in them. And as the globe slowly circled we saw the oceans and seas, some placid and others tossing and roaring, and here and there a ship. And all the life of Earth passed before our eyes.

We looked at this a long time, and our friend who belonged to this settlement spoke to us from below where we sat. He told us that what we were looking at was the Earth as it was at that moment. If we wished he would now show us the retroprogress of the ages from the present time to the beginning of man as an intelligent being. We replied that we would indeed be glad to see more of this wonderful and beautiful phenomenon, and he left us to go, I suppose, to the apparatus by which these things were controlled.

I may here pause to explain a matter which I see is in your mind. The place was not dark, it was light everywhere. But the globe itself shone with such extra intensity that, without any unpleasant sensation whatever, it obscured everything which was outside the blue cloud, which cloud seemed to be the circumference of the radiating beams shed by the globe.

Soon, then, the scenes began to change on the revolving sphere, and we were taken back through the thousands of years of the life of the Earth and the generations of men and animals and plant life which had been from the present to the ages when men were just emerging from the forest to settle in colonies on the plains.

Now, I must explain here that history was not followed as historians follow it. These phenomena were not of nations and centuries, but of aeons and species. The geologic periods passed before us, and it was intensely interesting to watch what men called the Iron Age and the Stone Age, the ice age, the floods, and so on. And those of us who understood enough to follow it noticed that these ages were rather arbitrarily named. For the ice age, for example, might correctly describe the state of things in one or two regions of the Earth, but there was by no means ice everywhere, as we saw as the sphere revolved. Also we noticed that very frequently one continent was in one age and another continent in another age at the same time. The exhibition ended, however, when the Earth was well progressed, and, as I have said, the advent of man was already an accomplished fact.

When we had satisfied our eyes for awhile looking on the beauty of this many-coloured and ever-changing jewel, and had realized that this was indeed no other than the old Earth we thought we knew so well, and found we knew so little, the globe gradually became smaller and floated back to the niche in the wall, and then the light faded out from it and it looked like an alabaster carving, just as we had seen it at first set there as an ornament.

We were so interested in what we had seen that we questioned our kind guide, and he told us many things about this hall. The Earth sphere which had just been used could be made to serve other purposes than the one we had seen. But that had been selected because its picturesqueness was suited to us who were not scientifically trained. Among other uses was that of illustrating the relation of the heavenly bodies one to another, and their evolution into their present state. In this, of course, the globe we had just seen played its appropriate part.

The animals about the walls were also used for a like purpose. One would be vivified by these powerful rays and brought forth into the centre of the hall. When so treated it could walk of itself like a live animal, which it was temporarily, and in a certain restricted way. When it had ascended a platform in the centre space, then it was treated with the enlarging rays—as I may call them, not knowing their scientific name—and then with others which rendered it transparent, and all the internal organism of the animal became plainly visible to the students assembled. Those who were of that settlement said that it was a very beautiful sight to see the whole economy of the system of animal or man at work so displayed.

Then it was possible to bring over the living model a change, so that it began to evolve backward—or should I say "involve"?—towards its simpler and primal state as a mammal, and so on. The whole structural history of the animal was shown in that life-like process. And often when the first period of its separate existence as a separate creature was reached, the process was reversed, and it passed through the different stages of development, this time in their correct order and direction, until it became again as it is to-day. Also it was possible for any student to take charge and continue the development according to his own idea, and this not of the animals alone, but of the heavenly bodies, and also of nations and peoples, which are dealt with in another hall, however, specially adapted to that study.

It was a student from one of these establishments, in this same region, who erected the globe in the children's garden, of which I told you.[16] But that is, of course, a much simpler affair, or so it appeared to us after visiting this colony of beauties and wonders.

That will have to suffice for this time, although there is a lot more we saw while there. But I must not start off again, or I shall be keeping you too long.

You have a question.

Yes, I was present on Monday at your Study Circle.[17] I knew she saw me, but could not make her hear me.

Good night, dear. We shall be with you to-morrow.

Monday, October 13, 1913

---

[16] See chapter 2.

[17] The reference to the Study Circle needs a note of explanation. It was on the previous Monday. I sat in the Sanctuary between the rails, and the members were facing each other in the choir stalls, Miss E. sat on my right at the Sanctuary end of the stall.

She afterwards told me that, when I was summing up the debate, she saw my mother step forth from the altar and come forward behind me with outstretched arms and a look of intense yearning and love on her face. She was exceedingly bright and beautiful, and her body looked as substantial as that of any of the others present. Miss E. thought she was going to clasp me in her arms, and it was so vivid that she forgot, for the moment, that the form was not of flesh and blood, and, therefore, could not be seen by the others.

She was on the point of crying out when she suddenly recollected herself, but had to look away in order to suppress her exclamation. It was about this I wished to ask the question.—G.V.O.

One more experience we had in that colony which you would like to hear about. It was one which was new to me and very interesting. We were being shown over the different establishments which formed a complete group, when we came to a kind of open-air pavilion. It was principally composed of a huge circular dome resting on tall pillars, and the interior space so enclosed was open to the air. In the centre of the platform to which we ascended by a flight of steps which were all round the building, was a kind of square altar some four feet high and three feet square. On this stood a bronze tablet, something like a sundial, marked with lines and symbols and different geometrical figures.

Above it in the centre of the dome was an opening which led, as we were told, into a chamber where the instruments used here were controlled.

We were told to stand round the dial (as I will call it) and our guide left us, and, going without, ascended to the roof of the dome, and so entered the chamber above us. We did not know what was going to happen, and so stood gazing at the disc.

Presently the place took on a different aspect, the air seemed to be changing in colour and intensity. And when we looked about us we saw that the landscape had disappeared, and between the pillars there stretched what appeared to be gossamer threads in the form of curtains. They were of various tints all interwoven, and, as we looked round, these seemed to separate into their own colours and then to take on more definite forms. This continued until we found ourselves standing in a glade with the circular belt of trees gently waving in the breeze.

Then birds began to sing, and we saw their bright plumage as they flew from one tree to another. Gradually we saw the distance deepen between the trees and could see far into a beautiful forest. The dome also was gone and the sky was above us, except where the trees stretched aloft like a canopy.

We turned again to the altar and the disc. These were still in place, but the figures and signs on the latter were now shining with a light which seemed to come from within the altar.

Now we heard the voice of our guide from above telling us to watch and try to read the tablet. We could make little of it at first, but at length one of our party more clever than the rest said that the signs were really representations of the various elements which went to make up the vegetable and animal bodies of the spiritual realms. It is difficult to explain the way in which the connection between the two was apparent to us. But when once pointed out it became quite clear that this was so.

Now our guide joined us once more and explained the use of the building. It seems that before the students are able to progress much in the science of creation as studied in this region, they have to get a thorough knowledge of the fundamental elements with which they have to deal. This is, of course, quite natural. This building is one of the first where they come to study, and the table, or dial, is a kind of register of these elements on which the student above in the chamber where the controlling instruments are can see the combination of elements he has brought about and also the proportion of each element entering into the combination.

Our guide was somewhat advanced in the science, and had contrived the forest scene by means of this same skill. As the learners progress they are able gradually to achieve the result they wish without the scientific apparatus which at first is necessary. One instrument after another is left out until at length they are able to depend solely on their will.

We asked our guide to what practical purpose the knowledge was put when acquired. He replied that the first use was the training of the mind and will of the student. That training was very excellent and very strenuous. When the student had become proficient he moved on to another college in this region where another branch of the science was learned, and then had to pass through many more stages of training. The actual use of his knowledge did not fall to his lot until he had passed through many spheres of progress. In the higher of these he was allowed to accompany some great Master, or Archangel, or Power (I do not know the exact and correct title) on one of his missions of service in the Infinite Creation of the One Father, and there witness the sublime process at work. It was thought that this might be the creation of some new cosmos or system, either material or spiritual. But that is so high above this state in which we are at present that we have only a general idea of the duties of those High Beings, and it is a matter of a few ages of progress from here to there, if our ways lie in the direction of that particular system of Heavens. And the chances are that, for us five women who visited the place I have been describing, our onward path will lead us somewhere else.

But we love to know all about the different spheres of service, even if we be destined never to be chosen for them. We cannot all be creators of cosmos, I suppose, and there are other things as necessary, great and glorious, no doubt, in those far reaches beyond us nearer to the Throne and Dwelling of Him Who is all in all to all.

As we returned across the wide grass-lands we were met by a party of these same students who had been to another college to study a different branch of science. They were not all men; some were women. I inquired if their studies were all on the same lines as that of their brothers, and they replied in the affirmative, but added that while the men students mostly looked after the purely creative part, they were permitted to add to and round off the work with their genius of motherhood, and that the two aspects blending enhanced the beauty of the finished work—finished, that is, so far as it was possible as conditioned by the limitations of their present spheres. For here were not so much spheres of perfect accomplishment as of progress towards those higher spheres.

By the time we had returned to the first colony where we had met our instructor of the circular estate——

Why do you not give me his name?

His name was Arnol,[18] but these names sound so strange to Earth ears, and people are always trying to find out their meaning, that we are rather shy of giving them. The meanings are mostly incomprehensible to you, so we will just say the name in future, as you wish it, and leave it there.

Well, it saves a lot of roundabout wording, doesn't it?

Yes, and yet if you understood the conditions under which we give you these narratives you would probably say that the longer was the more sure route. Remember our experience and teaching on Arnol's estate.

What makes it so difficult for you to give names? I have

---

[18] Arnol here referred to, for the first time, eventually communicated through the Rev. G. V. Owen a series of messages of a very high order, which are published in Volumes 3 and 4 of the Life Beyond the Veil. —H.W.E.

heard of this difficulty more than once.

There is also a difficulty in explaining the difficulty—from your point of view so apparently simple a matter. Let us put it in this way. You know that with the old Egyptians the name of a god or goddess was much more than a name as understood by the hardy materialistic Anglo-Saxon from whose race came the question: "What's in a name?" Well, from our point of view, and that also of the ancient wisdom of Egypt, based on data obtained from this side the Veil, there is a great deal in a name. Even in the mere repetition of some names there is actual power, and sometimes peril.

That we know now as we did not when on Earth. And so we here acquire a reverence for the entity "the Name," which to you would probably seem foolish. Nevertheless, it is partly for this reason that names do not come through to you so plentifully as many rather feeble investigators would wish.

Also the mere utterance and transmission of some of these names is, when we are in this Earth region, a matter of more difficulty than you would perhaps deem. It is a subject, however, which is hard to explain to you, and only one which you will be able to understand when you have become more familiar with the fourth dimension which obtains here—which term, also, we use for want of a better. We will just refer you to two or three instances and there leave the matter.

One is the giving to Moses of the Name of the great Officer of the Supreme who visited him. Moses asked for that Name, and got it—and neither he nor anyone else to this day has been able to say what it means.

Then the lesser Angel who came to Jacob. Jacob asked for his name, and it was refused him. The Angels who came to Abraham and to others in the Old Testament very seldom gave their names. Likewise in the New Testament, most of the Angels who come to minister to Earth's denizens are simply so called; and where the name is given, as in the case of Gabriel, it is little understood as to its inner significance. Of the new name which no man—that is, man on Earth—knoweth, we have already spoken.

What is your name, mother—I mean your new name? Is it permissible for you to give it?

Permissible, yes, but not wise, dear. You know I would give it if it were so. But this for the present I must withhold even from you, knowing that you will understand my love even if my motive is not very clear.

Yes, dear, you know what is best.

Some day you, too, will know, and then you will see what glory awaits those whose names are written in the Book of the Life of the Lamb, a phrase also which is worth thinking over, for in it is a glorious and living truth which those who use that Name so lightly surely apprehend little or not at all.

God bless you, dear, and Rose and the children. Ruby once more bids me in her pretty way, to say she is coming to see you soon, and hopes you will be able to take down her commands—that is the word she used, bless her, who is graceful humility itself, and loved by all who know her. God bless you, dear. Good-bye.

Wednesday, October 15, 1913.

How would you begin to explain to one who had little idea of a spirit world about him the truth of survival beyond the grave and the reality of this life and all its love and beauty? First you would probably endeavour to bring home to him the fact of his present actual existence as an immortal being. And then, when he had really grasped the significance of that, as it affects his future, he would perhaps be open to a few words of description as to that life which be will find himself possessed of, and in touch with, when he puts aside the Veil and emerges into the greater light of the Beyond.

So we feel that if men could but understand that the life they now live is life indeed, and not merely an ephemeral existence, they would then be more inclined to count worthy of consideration the words of those who have proved for themselves both the reality of this persistence of life and individuality, and also the blessedness of the lot awaiting those who on Earth are able to strive and to prevail.

Now, it is no small matter that men should so live their lives on Earth that when they step over the threshold into the larger, freer sphere they should take up and continue their service in the Kingdom without a more or less protracted hiatus in their progress. We have seen the effect of the career of so many, as it is viewed in extension into this land, that we feel we cannot too much emphasize the importance of preparation and self-training while opportunity offers. For so many do put off the serious consideration of this, with the idea of starting afresh here, and when they come over they find that they had very little realized what that starting afresh really implied.

Who is this writing?

Still your mother and her friends. Astriel is not here tonight, but will be with us on another occasion. We will let you know when it is he and his party communicating.

Well, to proceed then. We have already told you of the Bridge and the Chasm——

Yes. But what of your further experience in Arnol's domain, and of your return to your own proper sphere? Have you nothing more to tell me of that episode?

No more than that we learned much, made many friends, saw a great deal more than we here set down, and shall visit the place again soon. Now let us get on to what we wished to say, and which will perhaps be as useful as if we were to continue our description of the Colony in that other region.

The Chasm and the Bridge[19]—bring back your mind to what we told you of them. We wish to relate an episode which we witnessed at the place where the Bridge—as I will continue to name it—emerges on to the uplands of life and light.

We were sent thither to receive a woman who was expected to arrive, having fought her way through those dreadful, dark regions which lie below the Bridge. She had not come over the great causeway, but through the horrors of the darkness and gloom in the region below. With us went a strong Angel from a sphere above us, who was specially commissioned for the task. This was one of the Sister Angels who organize our homes where the rescued are taken.

Can you give me her name?

Bearn—no, we cannot get it through. Leave it, and we may be able to do so as we proceed.

When we arrived there we found that a light was glimmering some way down the rocky way which went down into the valley, and knew that some angel was there on the watch. Presently it grew more dim, and we noticed that it was moving

---

[19] See chapter 1.

away from us into the distance below. Then after a time we saw a flash far out over the valley, and this was immediately answered by a stream of light from one of the towers on the Bridge. It was not unlike what you know as a search light, and indeed answered a purpose somewhat similar. It shot out downward into the gloom and remained steady. Then Bea—our Angel Sister told us to abide where we were for a time, and she went quickly through the air to the tower top.

Then we lost her in the light, but one of my companions said she thought she saw her speeding along the ray of light which slanted downwards towards the depths. I did not; but afterwards we found that she had seen correctly.

I ought to pause here to explain that that light was not so much to enable the spirits to see (which they could do of their own power), but to give strength for the work and protection against the hurtful influences which held sway in the region below. It was for that reason that the first angel had sent out his signal, and it was understood by the constant watchers on the Bridge and answered in the way I have told. The ray of light is, in some way I do not understand yet, impregnated with power of life and strength—the best description I am able to give—and it was sent to help him whose strength was in want of succour.

By and by we saw the two return. He was a strong Angel, but looked fatigued, and we learned later that he had encountered a band of very malignant spirits who did their best to get the woman back again amongst them. That is why he needed help. He walked on one side and she walked on the other side of the poor torn and tortured soul who was more than half in a swoon. They went very slowly for her sake now, walking in the ray of light towards the tower on the Bridge. We had never seen anything like this before, except once, and that I have recounted to you. I mean the Pavilion of light and the assembling of the people of many coloured dresses. But this was, in a way, much more solemn; for here was anguish in the midst of joy, and there joy alone. They reached the Bridge, and the rescued one was taken into one of the houses and tended, and there remained until she had sufficiently recovered to be handed over to our care.

Now, there are several points in this narrative which held new knowledge for us, and some which confirmed what had been mere surmises up to the time of that experience. Some of these I will name.

It is a mistake to think that Angels, even of such estate as those two who went and rescued that poor woman, are unable to suffer. They do suffer, and that frequently. And it is possible for the malicious ones to hurt them when they venture into their regions. Theoretically I cannot see why the evil ones should not now and then prevail so as to get them into their power. So well, however, are the powers of light and good organized, and so watchful, that I have not heard that this catastrophe has ever been known actually to happen. But their fight is a real fight, and fatiguing also. That is the second point. Even these high Angels can become fatigued. But neither their suffering nor their fatigue do they mind. It may sound a paradox, but it is nevertheless true, that it is a joy to them to suffer so when some poor struggling soul is to be helped.

Also that light-ray—or perhaps I should say "ray of power and vitality"—was so strong that, had they not protected the woman by surrounding her with a certain negative influence, it would have harmed her, because it would have been too great a shock to one so unprepared as she.

Another point is this. That ray was seen far out in the region of gloom, and we heard a murmur coming, as it seemed, from hundreds of miles away, down across the valley. It was a strange experience, for the sound was that of many voices, and some were of rage and hate, and others of despair, and others cries for help and mercy. And these and other different cries seemed to be gathered each in its own particular locality, and to come from different directions. We could understand but little, but afterwards, while we waited for the rescued one, we asked Beanix—(I am afraid I cannot do better than that, so it will have to stand. We will call her Beanix, but it does not look quite correct when written down)—we asked her about those cries and where they came from. She said she did not know, but that there was provision for their registration, both collectively and individually, for their analysis, and that they would be scientifically treated in this science of love, and that then help would be sent out according to the merit of those who cried, and also in such form as would best be of service. Each cry was evidence either of good or bad in some human soul in that region, and would receive its appropriate answer.

When the woman was handed over to us we first let her rest and surrounded her with a quiet restful influence, and then, when she was strong enough, led her away to a home where she is being cared for and tended.

We did not ask her any questions, but let her ask the few she was able to put to us. But I found that the poor thing had been in that dark land for more than twenty years past. Her life history on Earth I have partly learned, but not enough to make a connected narrative. And it is not well to remind them too vividly at first of the Earth they have left so long ago. They usually have to work back from the present through their experience in the spirit life, in order to understand it and the relation of the whole—cause and effect, sowing and reaping—all explained.

That must serve for this time. Good-bye, dear, and God's blessing and our prayers shall be with and for you. May He keep you in His peace.

Amen.

Chapter 4

The City and Realm of Castrel

To the City and Realm of Castrel—The House of Castrel—Still-born children, not lost but gone before—Waters of life, Death and beyond death, no gap—Earth made perfect—The Manifestation in the old Council Chamber—Jolly Hooper interrupted—Traversing the spheres—"The Stars are the Angels"—The harp of light—The Summerland of God: its atmosphere—Departure from the City of Castrel—Wilfulness.

Friday, October 17, 1913

BY the time we had reached the Horne where we were charged to leave our poor sister, now so blessed, we were aware of another mission allotted to us. We were bidden to go to another district farther to the East.... You again hesitate, but that is the word we want. By the East we mean the direction from which the Brighter Light is seen over the mountains which border the plain where the Vision of the Christ and the Cross had been given to us. We often speak of that direction as the East because it reminds us of the Sunrise.

We set off, the five of us, all women, and kept before us the description we had received of the place we were to seek. We were to look for a great city among the mountains, with a golden dome in the midst of it, and the City itself surrounded by a colonnade on a terrace which ran round the City on all sides. We walked over the plain, and then went through the air, which requires more exertion, but is more speedy, and, in a case like ours, more convenient in enabling us to get a view of the country.

We sighted the City and descended before the principal gateway, by which we entered the main thoroughfare. It ran straight through the City and emerged through another gateway on the other side. On each side of this broad street there were large houses, or palaces, in spacious grounds, the residences of the principal officials of that district of which the City itself was the Capital.

As we came towards the City we had seen people working

in the fields, and also many buildings, evidently not residences, but erected for some useful purpose. And now that we were within the City walls we saw the perfection of both buildings and horticulture. For each building had a typical garden to match it both in colour and design. We passed on, waiting for some sign as to our destination and mission, for on such occasions as this a message is always sent on ahead, so that the visitors are expected.

When we had gone some way we entered a large square, where beautiful trees grew on lawns of the greenest of green grass, and fountains played a harmony together; that is to say, there were perhaps a dozen fountains, and each had a tone of its own, and each was composed of many smaller jets of water, each being a note. These are manipulated, on occasion, so that a fairly complicated piece of music can be played, with an effect such as that produced by an organ with many stops. At such times there are large numbers of people assembled in the square, or park, as I might call it, both of the citizens and also those who dwell outside among the hills and pastures. But when we came to it the fountains were playing a simple series of chords, in perfect harmony, and with most pleasing effect.

Here we lingered for awhile, for it is exceedingly restful and beautiful. We sat and lay upon the grass, and presently there came towards us a man who, by the smile on his face as he approached, we knew was the one who had been expecting us. We arose and stood before him in silence, for we did not feel inclined to begin the conversation, as we saw he was an angel of some degree considerably above us.

Please describe him, and give me his name if possible.

All in good time, dear. We learn to eliminate impatience here as a thing which confuses without adding impetus to the matter in hand.

He was tall—much taller than the average man on Earth I should say he would be some seven and a half feet high in Earth measurement. I am considerably taller than I was when with you, and he was much taller than I am. He wore a cream-coloured tunic, almost to his knees, bare arms and legs, and no sandals. You see I am answering what you are questioning in your mind. No, he had nothing on his head, but a beautiful veil of soft brown hair, parted in the middle and curling round his face and neck. One broad fillet of gold he wore, and in the centre and at the sides were set three large blue stones. He wore a belt of silver and some pink metal mingled, and his limbs shone with a soft glow. And these points, together with others, told us of his high degree.

There was also a calm benevolence and power in his firm but kindly countenance which gave both peace and trustfulness to us, as we stood before him, but also induced a reverence which we were glad to pay to one of such real worth as he.

He spoke at last, quietly, modulating his voice, as we instinctively knew, to our case. We could, nevertheless, detect the reverberating power in the tone of it. He said, "My name is Cast—". I am sorry. These names seem to be one of my weaknesses. They always perplex me when I try to reproduce them down here. But never mind his name for the moment. "I am C.," he said. "You have already heard of me from your own Superior, and now we meet in person. Now, my sisters five, come with me, and I will tell you why you have been sent to this City and to me." So we followed him, and on the way he chatted pleasantly, and we were quite at ease in his presence.

He led us down an avenue at right angles to the square, and then we emerged into another square; but we saw at once that this was a private square, and that the great palace, which lay away across the parklands before and around it, was the residence of some great Lord. We were guided through the park until we approached the great building, which stood, like some Greek temple, on a plateau which had a flight of steps on all sides of it.

The building was immense, and stretched before us, to right and left, and had high arches and entrances and porticoes, and surmounting it was a great dome. It was the landmark we had seen when approaching the City, only we found that it was not all gold, but gold and blue. We inquired who lived here, and he answered, "Oh, this is my home; that is, it is my city home; but I have also other houses out there in the country parts where I go from time to time to visit my friends whose duties lie in those districts. Come within and you shall be given the welcome which is your due, who have come so far to see us."

He spoke quite simply. I have come to know that here simplicity is one of the marks of great power. One might have thought that the proper way to usher one into the presence of a great noble would be to send servants to lead us to the Palace, and then that he should receive us in state. But they look at things differently here. No purpose would have served in this case by such ceremony, and so it was dispensed with. In cases where ceremony is helpful or desirable it is observed and sometimes with much grandeur. When it has no use it is not observed.

And that is how we came to the House of Castrel, —now you have his name as well as I am able to give it; of whom more another evening. You have to go now, so good night, dear, and all blessing to you and yours from these glowing and beautiful realms. Dear lad, good night.

Saturday, October 18, 1913

So he led us within, and we found that the interior of the house was lofty and very magnificent. The entrance-hall in which we stood was circular in shape, and open right up to the great dome above, which did not stand over the centre of the building, but receded a little from the portico over this entrance. The rotunda was richly embellished with stones of many colours, and hangings of silk-like texture, mostly of deep crimson. Doorways led off down long passages in front and on either side of us. Doves flitted about the dome itself, and evidently had means of ingress and egress. The material of which the arching roof of this dome was built was a kind of semi-opaque stone, and permitted the light to filter through in a softened glow. When we had looked about us for a time we found that we were alone, for Castrel had left us.

By and by, from down a passage on our right, we heard laughter and happy voices, and there presently emerged a party of women, with a few children among them. They numbered about twenty in all, and came to us, and took our hands in welcome, and kissed us on the cheek, and smiled on us, so that we were happier, if possible, than before. Then they drew away, and stood at a little distance, except one who had remained in the rear. She came forward and led us to a recess in the wall, where she bade us be seated.

Then, standing before us, she addressed each of us by name in greeting, and said, "You will wonder why you have come here, and what this City and place is to which you have been sent. This house in which you now are is the Palace of Castrel, as, no doubt, you already know. He is ruler of this wide district, where many occupations are followed, and many studies are pursued. I hear you have already been to the Colony of Music, and farther on to other settlements, where different branches of science are carried on. Now, we are in touch with all of these, and are constantly receiving their reports as to progress in this or that branch. These are considered and dealt with by Castrel and his officers, from the harmony point of view, as I will call it. Co-ordination, however, would express what I mean.

"For instance, a report will arrive from the College of Music, and another from that of Light, and another from the settlement where the Creative faculty is studied, and from other branches of service. These are all very carefully examined and analysed and tabulated, and, where necessity requires, the results are tested here, in one or other of the laboratories attached to this City. You will have seen some of these as you approached. They are scattered over the country to a great distance. They are not quite so complete in detail as those you have visited elsewhere, but, when any new apparatus is required, a mission is dispatched to inquire as to the construction, and these return and erect it in the spot most fitting in relation to the other establishments in this district; or perhaps it is added to the other apparatus already in existence in one or other of the buildings.

"You will understand, therefore, that an Overlord such as he who controls so varied a combination of knowledge must be well advanced in wisdom, and also is kept very busy at his work. It is this work you have been sent to see, and, while you remain with us, you will have ample opportunity of visiting some of the outlying stations. You will not, of course, understand all, or perhaps very much, of the scientific side of the work, but enough will be shown you to help you in your future work. Now come, and I will show you over this house, if you would care to see it."

We replied that we would, and thanked her for her kindness. So we went all over the principal parts of that magnificent dwelling. That is the only word I can find for it. Everywhere was colour blended with colour, bold but harmonious, and in such a way that, instead of being glaring, it had sometimes an exhilarating and sometimes a soothing and restful effect. Jewels and precious metals and beautiful ornaments, vases and pedestals and pillars—some standing alone as an ornament, each by itself, some in groups—hangings of glittering material which, as we passed through some doorway, swung into place again with a musical murmur, fountains with fish, courtyards open to the sky, in which grass and most beautiful trees and flowering shrubs grew, of such colours as are not known on Earth.

Then we ascended to the roof, and here again was a roof garden, but one of large extent, with grass and arbours and shrubs and fountains once again. It was mostly from this garden that messages and messengers were sighted; and also there were appliances by which correspondence could be carried on with distant regions by a kind of what you would perhaps call wireless telegraphy, but it was really different from that, inasmuch as the messages arrived in visible form mostly, and not in words.

In this mansion we stayed for a considerable period, and visited both the City and also the district around, a district which in Earth measure would be reckoned in thousands of miles across, but all in constant touch with the City and its communicating stations, and with this central Palace itself. Time would fail to tell you all. So I will just give you a few details, and leave you to imagine the rest, which, however, I know you will fail to do.

The first thing which puzzled me was the presence of children, for I had thought that all children were reared in special homes by themselves. The lady who had received us was the Mother of the place, and those who had attended her were some of her helpers. I asked one of these about these children who looked so happy and beautiful, and so perfectly at ease in this grand place. She explained that these were stillborn children, who had never breathed the atmosphere of Earth. For this reason they were of different character from others who had been born alive, even from those who had only lived a few minutes. They also required different treatment, and were able much sooner to imbibe the knowledge of these spheres. So they were sent to some such home as this, and were trained until they had progressed in mind and stature to such a degree that they were able to begin their new course of knowledge. Then, strong in heavenly purity and wisdom, they were taken in hand by those teachers who were in touch with the Earth itself, and were taught what they had not been able to learn before.

This was interesting to me, and presently I began to see that one reason I had been sent here was to learn this very thing, in order that there might be awakened in me by that knowledge the desire to know my own who had so passed into this land, and of whom I had not hoped to be called mother. O, the great and sweetest yearning which came to me when I realized this. I will not dwell upon it, but confess that for a time tears of unutterable joy dimmed my eyes at this one more blessing added to my already abundant store. I sat down on the grass beneath a tree, and hid my face in my hands, and bowed my head upon my knees, and there I remained helpless, from the too exquisite rapture, which filled and vibrated through my being till I shook all over. My kind friend did not speak to me, but sat down by my side, and put her arms around my shoulders, and let me sob out my joy.

Then, when I had somewhat recovered, she said very gently, "Dear, I also am a mother, the mother of one such as you will find here all your own. So I know what is in your heart at this moment, for I have experienced your present joy also."

Then I raised my eyes to her face, and she saw the question I could not ask her, and, taking my hand, she raised me, and, with her arm round my shoulder still, she led me towards a grove, where we heard children playing, their happy shouts and laughter coming through the trees—for I was very faint from all that great joy that filled me, and how should I sustain the greater joy to come?

Dear, that was not very long ago, and it is still so fresh to me that I find it hard to write for you clearly as I could wish. But you must forgive me if I seem to be too profuse, or too disjointed in my words. I had not known this truth, and when it was revealed to me so suddenly, and all the—to me—tremendous significance of it—well, I must leave you to try to understand. Suffice to say, I found in that glade what I did not know I possessed, and such a gift as this is more readily bestowed in this land than one is able with due self-control to receive.

I must add, before I cease, what I ought to have said before, but was carried on in spite of myself by the recollection of that sweet hour. It is this: When young children come over here they are first schooled in this life and then have to learn what experience they have lacked on Earth. The more training they have acquired in the Earth life, the sooner they are sent to complete it. Those who are stillborn have had no Earth training at all. Nevertheless, they are children of the Earth and, as such, they must return and acquire it. Not until it is safe for them to do so, however, and then under proper guardianship until they are competent to go alone. Their return to the neighbourhood of the Earth sphere is consequently longer delayed, and one who has lived a long and busy life on Earth has less to learn of Earth life when he comes over here, and so can pass on to other and higher studies.

Of course, these are only the broad governing principles, and, in application to individuals, account has to be taken of personal characteristics, and the rule modified and adapted as the particular case requires or merits.

But all is well for all who live and love, and those who love best live the loveliest life. That sounds rather too alliterative, but let it stand, for it is true. God bless you, dear. Good night.

Monday, October 20, 1913.

We were walking down the principal street of that beautiful city on a tour of inspection. We wanted to understand why it was laid out in so many squares, and what was the use of some of the buildings we had noticed on both sides of that broad way. When we had arrived at the farther gateway, we saw that the City stood very high above the surrounding plains. Our guide explained that the reason for this was that those on the towers might see as far as possible, and also might be seen by those in the distant settlements of this district. This was the Capital City of the region, and all business going on found its focus here.

On our way back we visited several of the buildings, and were everywhere kindly received. We found few children, other than those in Castrel's Home. Here and there, however, there were groups in the squares, where the fountains played and were surrounded by basins into which their waters fell. These were all connected with one broad stream which issued forth from one side of the City, and fell into the plain below, a brilliant waterfall of many tints and of sparkling brightness. It took its way across the plain, a fairly broad stream flowing gently over the sands, and we saw, here and there, some children bathing in it, and throwing it over their beautiful bodies in great enjoyment. I did not think much of this until my guide remarked that these children were encouraged to bathe in the waters, as they were electrically charged, and gave strength to them, for many came here very weak and required such nourishment.

I expressed my surprise at this, and she replied, "But what would you have? You know that, although not of material flesh and blood, yet our bodies here are solid and real as those we have laid aside. And you know that these bodies of our present state correspond to the spirit within much more accurately than those others used to do. Now these little spirits are, most of them, only beginning to develop and need bodily nourishment to help them on the way. Why not?"

Why not, indeed! Surely I was slow to learn all that that phrase I have already given you implied, "Earth made perfect." I fear many of you when you come over here will be much shocked to see how very natural all things are, even if more beautiful than on the Earth. So many expect to find a vague shadowy world over here, totally diverse from Earth in every possible way. And yet, come to think of it, and with common sense, what good would such a world be to us? It would not mean a gradual progress for us, but a vast leap, and that is not the way of God.

Things here when first we arrive are certainly different from those of the old life, but not so different as to make us feel dumbfounded by their strangeness. Indeed, those who come over after living an unprogressive life on Earth, find themselves in spheres of so gross a character as to be, to them, indistinguishable from Earth itself. That is one of the reasons why they are not able to realize that they have changed their state. As you progress through the lower spheres into the higher, this grossness gradually gives place to more rare conditions, and the higher you go the more sublimated is the environment. But few, if any, pass into those spheres where no trace of Earth is seen, or no likeness to the Earth life. I doubt if, as a rule, any do. But of this I must not speak dogmatically, for I have not myself reached, or even visited, a sphere where there is absolutely no likeness to God's beautiful Earth. For it is beautiful, and we have to learn its beauties and wonders here, as part of our training. And, learning so, we find that Earth is but one further manifestation outward from our own spheres, and in tune with us and our present environment in many very intimate ways. Were it not thus we could not be communing with you at this moment.

Also-and I merely say this as it appears to me who am not very wise in these things—I do not see how people passing over from the Earth life into this could possibly get here were there a great gap between us, a gigantic void. How could they cross it? But that is simply my own thought, and there may be nothing in it at all. Only of this I am fairly certain: if people would but keep in mind the Oneness of God and His Kingdom, and the gradual progression which, in His wisdom, He has ordained for us, then they would much better understand what death is and what is beyond. It would probably be utterly absurd to many to be told that here we have real solid houses and streets and mountains and trees and animals and birds; and that animals are not here for ornament alone, but also for use; and that horses and oxen and other animals are put to use. But they enjoy their work in a way which makes one glad to watch them. I noticed a horse and rider coming along the street once, and I wondered which was enjoying the canter the more of the two. But I fear this will not be accepted by many, so I will get on to another theme.

One of the buildings in the broad street was a library where records were kept of reports from the outlying stations. Another was a laboratory where some of the reports could be tested by actual experiment. Another was a lecture hall where professors gave their results to those of their own and other branches of science. Another had a somewhat curious history.

It stood well back from the street and was built of wood. It looked like polished mahogany, with streaks of gold in the grain. It was erected long ago as a Council Chamber for the Chief of that time, long before Castrel took over the work. Here he used to assemble the students in order that they might each give an exhibition of their knowledge in practical form.

A young man arose on one occasion, and, going to the centre of the auditorium, stood there and stretched out his hands, and remained facing the President. As he stood there his form seemed to change and become more radiant and translucent, until at last he was surrounded by a large halo of light, and there were seen about him many Angels from the higher spheres. His smile had some enigma in it which the Prince was trying to read, but could not. Just as he (the Prince or Chief) was about to speak, there came through the open door a little boy-child, and looked round in surprise at all the great crowd.

He paused at the edge of the circle and looked on the multitude of faces of those who sat there in tiers, one above the other, round the circle, and seemed abashed. He was just turning to run away again when he caught sight of the one who stood in the centre, now glowing with light and glory. Immediately the little lad forgot everybody else, and, running as fast as his little legs would carry him, he went straight to the centre of the circle with outstretched hands and a look of great joy in his face.

The one who stood there then lowered his arms, and, stooping down, took up the little one and laid him on his shoulder, and then, approaching the Prince, he gently laid the little fellow in his lap and began to walk back towards the place where he had stood. But as he went his form grew dim, and, before he had reached the spot he had left, he had become quite invisible, and the whole space was empty. But the little boy lay in the Prince's lap, and looked up into his face—a very beautiful face it was—and smiled.

Then the Prince arose, and, holding the child on his left arm, he reverently laid his right hand on his head, and said, "My brothers, it is written, 'A little child shall lead them,' and these words come to my mind but now. What we have seen is a Manifestation of our Lord the Christ, and this little one is of those who are of the Kingdom, as He said. "What message did He give you, child, as you lay in His arms, and He brought you to mine?"

Then for the first time the boy spoke and said, with a child's accent, and still very shy of the large audience, "If you please, Prince, I must be good and do as you instruct me, and then He will show me, from time to time, new things for your City and Realm. But I don't know what it means."

Nor did the Prince, nor the students at first. But he dispersed them and took the little one home to his own house, and thought the matter out. He came to the conclusion it was Eli and Samuel over again, without the more unpleasant details. As a matter of fact, as it turned out, he had read the matter correctly. The child was allowed to play about the laboratories and scientific schools, and watch and listen. He never was in the way, and did not bother them with questions. But now and again, when some extra-difficult piece of work was on hand, he would make some remark, and when he did so, it was always the key to the solution. Also—and this was considered, as time went on, to be the principal object He had in giving that Manifestation—the students learned simplicity; that is, that the simpler the solution they could find to any problem in particular, the better it fitted into the general scheme with other solutions.

There were many other lessons also which they learned from the Vision itself; for instance, the fact that His Presence was among them always, and that at any time He might become visible, for, when He came that time, He walked out from among the assembly of students. Also, the outstretched arms taught them of self-sacrifice even in those happy realms where glories shone about them, even as it had shone about His form as He stood there. But the child: he grew as His Divine Sponsor had grown, in wisdom and stature, and when the Prince of that time was taken into a higher sphere, he succeeded him in his high office.

Well, all this is long ago, and still the old hall stands to-day. It is always kept carefully tended and made beautiful without and within with flowers. But it is not used now for lectures and discussions, but for service of worship. One of the artists of the City made a painting of the scene, and that was placed there behind the Altar, like many on Earth. And from time to time worship is offered to the Great Father of all, in the sanctifying Presence of His Anointed Son, and, on some of the greater occasions, the Prince who was there when that Vision was given will descend from the higher spheres with the little boy, now a great Angel-Lord, and others who have held the office since their time; and those who assemble there know that some great blessing and Manifestation will be given. But only those who are fitted by their developed state are present at such times, for the Manifestation would not be visible to those who have not reached a certain stage in progress.

God's spheres are wonderful in their beauty of light and glory; but most wonderful of all seems the Presence of His Spirit through all these infinities and eternities, and His tender love to all, both wise and simple; and to you and me, dear, in that He has so ordained the co-operation of the different estates within His Realm that we can talk together thus, you and I, dear, through the thin Veil which hangs between.

Tuesday, October 21, 1913.

Of that city I could tell you much more than I have done. But I have other matters to deal with, and will, therefore, give you just one more item of our life there and then pass on to other things.

We were lodging in a cottage within the Palace grounds where the children often came to see us, and my own little one among them. They seemed to be glad to come and see their little friend's mother and her fellow visitors, and were never tired of hearing about the other places we had visited, and especially the children's homes and schools. They would weave garlands of flowers and bring them to us as gifts, with the hope at the back of their minds that we would in return join them in one of their games. This we often did, and you will easily imagine how I enjoyed those romps with these dear little children in that quiet and peaceful place.

We were once playing with them at a game they had invented among themselves, a kind of jolly Hooper game such as you used to play, and we had won nearly all the others on to our side, when the few who were left facing us suddenly stopped in their song and stood still, looking beyond us. We all turned round, and there, standing in the entrance of a long avenue of trees at the edge of the glade, was no other than Castrel.

He stood there smiling at us, and, although his aspect was so kingly, yet there were so much gentleness and humility blended with his strength and wisdom, that he was very lovely to look upon, and to be near. He came slowly forward and the children ran to him, and he patted one and another on the head as he came. Then he spoke to us. "You see," he said, "I knew where I might find you, and so I needed no guide. And now I am obliged to cut your play short, my sister-visitors, for there is a ceremony on hand at which you ought to be present. So you little ones must continue your games alone while these big children come with me."

Then they ran to us and kissed us happily, and made us promise to come and continue our games as soon as we were at liberty.

So we followed the Prince Castrel along the avenue of trees which formed a leafy tunnel meeting overhead. We walked to the end and emerged into the open country, and here our guide paused and said, "Now I want you to look yonder and tell me what you see!"

We, one and all five of us, told him we saw a large undulating plain, with many buildings here and there, and, beyond, what appeared to be a long range of high mountains.

"Nothing else?" he asked.

We replied that we could see nothing else of importance, and he continued, "No, I suppose that is about the limit of your vision at present. But my sight, you see, is more developed than yours, and I can see beyond those mountains yonder. Now listen, and I will tell you what I see. Beyond that range I see other mountains higher still, and beyond them still more lofty peaks. On some of these are buildings, others are bare. I have been in that region also, and I know that among those mountains, which from this point are viewed foreshortened, are plains and tracts of country as wide as this of which this City is the chief.

"I am now looking at the shoulder of a mountain, not on the horizon, as I see it, but far beyond your own range of vision, and I see a large and glorious City, much more extensive and much richer and more magnificent than this. The principal gateway fronts in this direction, and before it is a large flat space. Through this gateway are emerging horses and chariots with drivers, and other horses with riders. They have now assembled and are about to start. Now their leader emerges from the crowd and comes to the front. He gives an order and the crowd of citizens raise their hands and wave a God-speed to them. Now their Prince moves forward to the edge of the cliff on which the City is erected. He leaves the edge and proceeds by aerial flight. His chariot leads the way and the others follow. And they come," he added with a smile, "in this direction. Now we will go to another place, and you shall witness their arrival."

None of us asked the reason of their visit. It was not that we were afraid to do so. I think we could have asked him anything. But we somehow felt that all that it was meet that we should know then had been told us, and so we were content to wait. But he said, "You are curious to know the reason of their coming. That you will shortly be permitted to see." So we went with him to the wall of the City, and stood there looking over the plain towards the hills. We could see no more than we had said.

"Tell me," he said, "which of you first sights them."

We looked long and eagerly, but could not see anything. At last I thought I saw a star begin to twinkle over the mountains far away in the depths of space. Just at that moment one of my companions exclaimed, "I think, my lord, that star was not there when first we came here."

"Yes," he replied, "it was there, but not visible to you. So you are the first to see it?"

I did not like to say I had seen it also. I should have said that before. But he continued, "I think there is someone else who sees that star. Is that not so?" and he turned to me with a quiet smile. I am afraid I reddened and mumbled something awkwardly. "Well," he said, "watch it. You others will also be able to see it presently. At this moment it is several spheres away, and I did not expect any of you to be able to see quite into that region." Then, turning to us two, he bowed courteously, and said, "Ladies, I congratulate you on your good progress. You are rapidly advancing towards a higher grade, and if you continue, your sphere of service will soon be enlarged, believe me." We were both made very happy by this speech.

But now the star had considerably brightened, and even, as we looked, it seemed to enlarge and expand, and this continued a long space of time. Then I noticed that it was no longer a round disc, but was gradually assuming another shape, and, at last, I was able to see what the shape was. It was a harp of light, somewhat in the shape of a lyre, and seemed to be like a jewel set with many diamonds. But as it came nearer and nearer, we were able to see that it was made up of horses and chariots and men, and that in that order they were speeding through space towards us.

Presently we heard shouts of welcome from the people on other parts of the City walls and knew that they had sighted them also.

"Now you see the nature of their business in this City."

"Music," I suggested.

"Yes," he answered, "it has to do with music. That is the main object of this visit, anyway."

As they drew nearer we saw that the company numbered some hundreds. It was a beautiful sight to see. There they came along the path of the heavens, horses and chariots of fire—you know the old familiar phrase; believe me, it is little understood—with riders of light radiating their glory far around them, as they sped along their heavenly way. O, these citizens of those higher realms are all too beautiful for us to describe to you. The lowest in rank of these was just about of Castrel's degree. But his own glory was constrained and hidden, in order that he might be both Prince of this City and also a citizen. Yet, as his companions and peers drew near, we noticed that he also began to change. His face and form glowed with an ever-increasing radiance until, at length, he shone as bright as the least bright of those who came along the sky. I could understand, when I thought of it afterwards, why it was necessary for him to condition himself to the lower sphere in which he served. For, as he stood before us now, even though he had not attained the full intensity of his native brightness, yet none of us dared approach him, but drew a little distance away, and left him to stand alone. We were not afraid, but unaccustomed—that is as well as I can put it.

The members of the flashing jewelled harp at last were speeding over our own country, and when they had come half the way between us and the first range of hills, they slowed down and gradually reformed. This time the band took the shape of a....[20] Then sweeping down they landed on the space before the principal gate of the City.

Castrel had left us for some time now, and, as they landed, we saw him issue on foot from the City gate, attended by his principal men. He was robed in light—that is nearly all I could see. But the diadem he wore shone more brilliantly than I had ever seen it; and so did the girdle he wore. He approached the leader and knelt before him. This Angel was much brighter even than Castrel. He descended from his chariot and, hastening to our own Prince, lifted him up and embraced him. The action was full of grace and also of love, and, for the few seconds they were together, there was complete silence on the walls. But when the embrace was done, and the words of blessing—in a language we do not understand—were spoken, Castrel bowed his head before the other and then, standing up, looked to the City walls and raised his hand, and there was a burst of music and voices as the citizens broke into a glorious anthem. I have told you of the singing in another region. This was much more sublime, for this was a plane in advance of that. Then they too, followed by the other visitors, entered the City amidst the shouts of the populace and the pealing of bells and strains of instrumental music and the singing of the thousands upon the walls.

So they passed along the street to the Palace, and, as he turned into the avenue which led off the main street, the Angel

---

[20] See further on in this chapter.

Prince, our visitor, halted, and, standing in his chariot, turned round, and, lifting his hand, blessed the people in their own tongue, and then went on down the avenue and was, with his glittering attendants, lost to view.

Dear, I have tried my very best to give you even a faint description of that incident. I have failed miserably. It was much more glorious than I have been able to describe. I have spent my time also on the description of this arrival scene because that I could understand better than the mission on which they had come. That is far too deep for me, and concerned the teachers of the City and the great men of that land. All I could get to know was that it was chiefly concerned with the studies of the most advanced in that Colony of the connection of music with the creative faculty. I cannot understand more than that. But perhaps others will be able to say more about it than I can.

That word we could not give above was "planet" the second formation, we mean—not "planet,"[21] but "planetary systems." I do not know whether it was the solar system, of which the Earth is a unit, or other—some other system I rather think; but I do not know.

That is all, dear, tonight. Are you waiting for our blessing? God bless you, dear lad. Lift up your eyes and keep your ideals bright, and believe that the most glorious of glories you can imagine are to the real and actual glories of this life of ours just as candle light to that of a sun.

Wednesday, October 22, 1913.

If all the world were one great diamond or pearl reflecting or radiating the light of the sun and distant stars, how bright would be its vicinity. Yet in a measure it does this, but only to a very limited degree because of the lack of lustre on its surface. And as the reflecting capacity of the Earth is to that more perfect mirror which a pearl would furnish, so is the Earth life to ours here in these realms of light and beauty, the Summerland of God.

As we gaze out over the wide plains and valleys of the Heavenly Land, we are scarce able to remember the effect of the

---

[21] See further back in this chapter.

atmosphere of Earth as it had relation to our vision of terrestrial things. But we do remember certain qualities which here are absent. Distance is not obscured, for instance. It fades away. Trees and plants do not appear for a season, and then die. They bloom perpetually, and then, when plucked, they are fresh for a long time, but they do not droop and wither. They, too, fade, or melt, away into the atmosphere. This same atmosphere is not always white. In the neighbourhood of the City of the Prince Castrel there is a sense of golden sunshine all around. It is not a mist, and does not obscure, but bathes all things in its golden radiance without invading the various colours themselves. In other places it is of a faint pink or blue. And every region has its own peculiar tint, or sense, of colour, according to the nature of the people and their employment and bent of mind.

The tint of the atmosphere seems to be governed by this principle; but also it is reflex in its action on the people themselves. Especially is this the case with visitors from other regions. The more highly developed, on coming into a new tract of country, are able to tell by this alone the general character and occupations of the people there. The influence, however, very quickly extends to themselves. It does not change them in character, of course, but it does affect their sensations, and is almost instantaneously seen in the changing hue of their robes.

Thus, as one visits a strange district, one very speedily begins to feel, within and without, that sense of brotherhood and sisterhood which is one of the most delightful of blessings I have found. Everywhere you go you find brothers and sisters. Try to think of it and see what it would mean if it were thus on Earth. Then the Angels' greeting of Peace and Goodwill indeed would be realized and Earth would be the ante-chamber of the Heavenly Home.

We returned from that City asking ourselves what difference our visit had made in us, and what we had learned. For my own part, it was not difficult to see that the very fact of my own little girl being there was enough. She is a gift I had not expected. But as we returned leisurely across the plain, we found that each had received some special blessing for herself alone.

As we had approached the City by the air, we preferred now to go afoot across the plain until we reached the mountains. And as we went we talked of what we had seen. Now, I could fill many pages with that talk, and I assure you it would not be uninteresting. But time and space are to you, and to publishers, of more account than they are to us, so I will hasten on to what I have to tell.

We reached our own sphere just as our Mother Angel had also returned from a journey to the Bridge of which I have already told you. She brought with her this time one you know.

Name, please.

Mrs. S. She had been through a rather trying experience. When first she came over she was taken to a place where she might have progressed rapidly. Hers was a perplexing case; so many mixed traits that it was very difficult to place her exactly. So she was given the chance and helped in every way. But, you must know, freewill and personality are very important things here, and are never overruled when help is being offered. She soon grew restless, and it was seen that she would have to be given her way. So she was warned and advised and then taken to the parting of the ways to choose her own road, as she wished to do. A guardian was appointed to keep constant watch in order that if help were sought any time it would be near at hand.

Well, she did not seem to know where to go or what to do, to find what she wanted—peace. So she wandered on and spent a considerable period in the neighbourhood of the Bridge. It was only when she had learned for herself that her own wilful course led again and again into places where the darkness always increased, and people, sights and sounds were of a nature not to radiate happiness, but sometimes terror, that at last she wandered along the borderland, and, by and by, turned a little towards the light and was gradually helped back again to the Home she had left. She is now progressing, slowly, to be sure; but still with an ever softening heart, and more humility and trust, and she will do well in time. That is why I have seen so little of her, and been of so little use. But I may be able to help a little now and again as time goes on. Perhaps that is why she has been brought to the place where I am destined to spend a more or less protracted period of service. I did not know her in the Earth life except through you, and your friendship with her children may be the link which will enable her to receive any little help I am able to give.

You see, everything is considered here, even the things which seem so casual and transitory in the Earth life. They are all registered and viewed in their relation to one another, all the seemingly casual talks or chance meetings, a book read, a hand shake in the street for the first time and never again, a few friends meeting, in the same way, at a mutual friend's house and never meeting again—everything and every item is registered, considered, co-ordinated and used when, and if, occasion offers. And so may it be in this case.

Be, therefore, not remiss to weigh well all you do and every word you say; not in anxiety, but rather by cultivating a habit of will to do good; always and everywhere to radiate kindness of heart, for in the Kingdom these are not of small account, but go to make robes bright and bodies radiant.

And so, dear, good night once again—a wish not without its significance to you, if otherwise to us, for here all is good to them who goodness love, and night is absent always where the True Light shines forever, and all is Peace.

Chapter 5

Angelic Ministry

Another from the Bridge—Conscience—The Judgment—Self-delusion—Difficulties and hindrances in communication through the Veil—"Set a watch, O Lord, before my mouth; keep the door of my lips"—The method of impression—A meeting in the air—Not motherless—A mixed character.

Thursday, October 23, 1913

PERCHANCE if we were to tell you of our progress in these heavenly spheres we should weary you, for much detail has to be negotiated, and nothing passed over as being too small. But it may be helpful if we supplement what we wrote in this vein last evening by giving you now an instance by way of illustration of this point.

We received a message a short time ago of the arrival of a sister at the Bridge, who had come over from the further side where lie the regions of gloom, and I and another were sent to conduct her to this Home. We went quickly and found our charge awaiting us. She was quite alone, for her attendants had left her thus in order that she might profit by a quiet period of meditation and reflection before beginning her further advance.

She was seated on a slope of grass under a tree whose branches spread like a canopy over her. Her eyes were closed, and we stood before her waiting. When she opened them she looked at us for some time in an inquiring manner. As she did not speak, I at last addressed her "Sister." At that word she looked at us hesitatingly, and then her eyes began to fill with tears, and she put her face in her hands, bowed her head upon her knees, and wept bitterly.

So I went to her and laid my hand upon her head and said, "You are our sister now, dear, and as we do not weep, so neither must you."

"How do you know who or what I am?" she replied, as she raised her face and tried to force back her tears, while there was just a touch of defiance in her voice.

"We do not know who you are," I answered. "What you were we do know. We know that you were always a child of our Father, and so, always our sister. Now you are our sister in a fuller sense. What else you are lies with you. You are either one whose face is set toward the Sunshine of His Presence, or one who, fearing the task before you in that direction, will turn back again across the Bridge."

She was silent for a while, and then said, "I dare not. It is all too horrible over there."

"But," I urged, "you must choose; for you cannot remain where you are. And you will come the upward way—will you not?—and we will lend you a sister's hand and give you a sister's love to help you on the way."

"Oh, I wonder how much you know of what lies yonder," she said, and there was agony in her voice. "There they called me sister, too; they called me sister in mockery, while they heaped upon me infamy and torture and—oh, I must not think of it or it will drive me mad again. But I don't know how I shall proceed; I am so stained and vile and weak."

But I saw that this would never do, so I cut her short. I told her that, for the present, she must try to forget these experiences, until we had helped her, and then it would be time enough to begin her task in earnest. I knew that task was going to be a heavy and bitter one; but there is only one way onward, nothing can be glossed over; everything must be viewed and understood for exactly what it is—every act and word up to the present time—God's justice acknowledged, and God's Love through all—and that is the only onward and upward way. But that must rest a while until she was capable of enduring it. And so we comforted her and gradually led her away.

Now, as we went she began to look around and ask about the things she saw, and what kind of country lay ahead, and what the home was like to which she was being led, and so on. We told her all she could understand. We told her of our Angel Mother who had charge of the place, and of our fellow-workers there. In the midst of our conversation she stopped suddenly and said she felt she could go no further. "Why?" we inquired, "are you tired?" and she answered, "No; afraid."

We saw something of what was in her mind, but could not quite understand it as a whole. There was something we could not lay hold of. So we led her on to talk of herself, and at last we unearthed the difficulty.

It seems that when the guardian at the other end of the Bridge had heard her cry for help far away in the gloom, he at once directed a ray of his light in the direction, and sent a messenger to help her. This spirit found her fainting by the side of a dark murky stream whose waters were foul and hot, and bore her to the Bridge Gatehouse. Here she was tended and revived and brought forward across the Bridge to the place where we found her.

Now it chanced that when this spirit worker had found her she had felt a presence but could not see any one near. She therefore called aloud, "May you be cursed if you touch me!" thinking that perhaps it was one of her old tormentors and companions in wickedness. Then she remembered no more until she recovered her senses again in the Gatehouse. As we walked and talked of the workers of these realms the memory of that incident suddenly came back to her mind. She had cursed one of God's ministers, and she was afraid of the light because the words were evil. Truly, she did not know whom she had cursed; but a curse is a curse against whomsoever directed, and it lay upon her heart.

My companions and I consulted together briefly and came to the conclusion that we must return. The other sins of this poor soul might be dealt with presently. This, however, was against one of our fellow-workers of the realms of light and love, and we saw that she would find no rest among us, and our services would little avail her until that wrong had been righted. So back to the Bridge we went, and right across it to the Gatehouse at the further end.

There we found the spirit helper who had brought her to that place, and she asked and obtained forgiveness. Indeed, he was awaiting us; for he was stronger and more progressed than we, and so was greater in wisdom, and he knew that she would compel herself to return. So as we drew near he came from the gateway where he had been standing watching us coming along the road, and, when she saw his kind face and forgiving smile, she knew at once it was he whom she sought and, falling on her knees, obtained his blessing.

I fear this is not a very exciting message tonight. I have given it to show you how even the seemingly slight things have to be reckoned with here. As a matter of fact, I believe that some higher intelligence than our own was controlling us all the time; for that little incident proved a very important episode in the progress of that poor sinful woman. It was a long journey back to, and across, the Bridge, and she was very weak and weary. But when she saw the face of the one against whom she had sinned, and heard his words of love and forgiveness, it showed her, for the first time, that whatever she should have to endure in future it would be sweet in the end, and each task done would earn its own blessing. And that is no mean support to such as she who had so much to face of repentance and agonizing shame of remembrance of the Great Love of God which she had flouted and denied.

What is she doing now?

That was not very long ago, and she has been progressing but slowly. There is so much to keep her back. But she does progress, nevertheless. She is in our Home, but has not yet been given any special work to do for others. She will be so employed eventually, but not for a long time to come.

Sin may be negative in its essential parts, but it is negation of the Love and Fatherhood of God, and that is a far more terrible thing than mere offence against a commandment. It is the contamination of the very nature and spring of our inner spirit life, of the Sanctuary of the Spirit of God. And the cleansing of a polluted Sanctuary is more than the washing of an ordinary dwelling. The very intensity of the Light of the Presence in this spiritual state shows up every speck and mote, and happy are those who keep that Sanctuary clean and bright, for such shall know how sweet it is to live and to love in Him.

Monday, October 27,1913.

Once again we take up our tale of the Heavenly Life, and hope to be able to tell you a little more of the love and blessedness which we experience in these bright realms. Our Home is situate on the slope of a thickly-wooded hill in a clearing, and our patients—for they are really such—are tended by us here in peace and quiet after their distressing experiences in one or other part of those lands where the light is dim, and darkness seems to enter into their very souls. They come here more or less exhausted and weak, and are only allowed to go onward when they have become strong enough for the way.

You would perhaps like to know somewhat of our methods here. Chiefly these may be summed up in one word: Love. For that is the guiding principle in all our work. Some are so overjoyed with the realization of the fact that we do not seek to judge and punish, but only to help them, that they are, from that very cause, ill at ease from its unfamiliarity.

One of our poor sisters met our Mother Angel a little while ago in the garden, and was turning down a side-path in order to avoid meeting her, not of fear but of reverence. But our bright Angel went to her and spoke kindly to her, and when she found she could talk quite freely she asked a question. "Where is the judge," she inquired, "and when is the judgment to take place? I am trembling all the while with the thought of it, for I know my punishment will be a very dreadful one; and I would know the worst, and get it over."

To this the Mother replied, "My child, your judgment will take place whenever you desire; and from your own words I can tell you that it has already begun. For you own that your past life is worthy of punishment, and that is the first step in your judgment. As to the judge, well, she is here; for you yourself are judge, and will mete out to yourself your punishment. You will do this of your own free will by reviewing all the life you have lived and, as you bravely own up one sin after another, so you will progress. Much of your punishment you have already inflicted upon yourself in those dark regions from which you have lately come. That punishment, indeed, was dreadful. But that is past and over, and what you have now to endure will be dreadful no longer. All dread should now be past. Painful, deeply painful, I fear it will be. But all through you will feel that He is leading you, and this more and more as you go on in the right way."

"But," persisted the inquirer, "I am perplexed because I do not see the Throne of the Great judge who will reward some and punish others."

"You will, indeed, some day see that Throne, but not yet. The judgment you are thinking of is very different from what you imagine. But you should have no fear and, as you progress, you will learn more, and understand more, of God's great love."

That is what perplexes many who come over here. They expect to find all set ready for their dismissal from the Presence into torture, and cannot understand things as they are.

Others who have cultivated a good opinion of their deserts are much disappointed when they are given a lowly place, sometimes a very lowly one, and not ushered immediately into the Presence of the Enthroned Christ to be hailed with His "Well done." Oh, believe me, dear son, there are many surprises awaiting those who come over here, some of a very joyful kind, and others the reverse.

I have, only lately, seen a very learned writer, who had published several books, talking to a lad who, in the Earth life, was a stoker in a gasworks, and being instructed by him. He was glad to learn, too, for he had partly learned humility; and the curious thing was that he did not so much mind sitting at the feet of this young spirit as going to his old friends here and owning up his mistakes and his vanity of intellect in his past life. This, however, he will have to do sooner or later, and the young lad is preparing him for the task. It is also whimsical to us to see him still clinging to his old pride, when we know all about him, and his past and present status, which latter is rather low, and all the time he is trying to think he is hiding his thoughts from us. With such their instructors have to exercise much patience, which is also very good training for them.

And now let us see if we can explain a difficulty which is perplexing many investigators into psychic matters. We mean the difficulty they have in understanding why we do not give them information which they desire about one thing or another which they have in their minds.

You must try to realize that when we come down here we are not in our proper element, but are hampered with limitations which are now strange to us. For instance, we have to work according to the laws which are in vogue in the Earth realm, or we could not make you understand what we wish to do or say. Then we often find that when any one has his mind fixed on some particular person whom he wishes to hear or see, or some special matter about which he wishes to inquire, we are limited by the straitened means at our disposal. Other reservoirs of power in that inquirer are closed, and those only are open to us which he himself has willed should be open. And these are frequently not enough for us to work with.

Then again, the activity of his will meets the activity of ours midway, as it were, and there is a clash, and the result is either confusion or nil. It is nearly always better to allow us to work in our own way, trustfully, and afterwards to examine critically what we manage to get through. If information on any particular point is desired, let that point be in your mind at times as you go about your daily occupation. We shall see it and take account of it, and, if it is possible and useful and lawful, we shall find opportunity and means, sooner or later, to answer it. If you ask a question while we are with you manifesting in one way or other, do not demand, but just put your thoughts before us, and then leave it to us to do what we can. Do not insist. You may be sure that, as our desire is to help, we shall do all we can.

And now to a case in point. You have been wanting to know about Ruby and others. You have not insisted, and, therefore, we have been able to use conditions freely and are able to give you some information.

Ruby is happy as ever, and getting quite expert in the work she has in hand. I saw her only lately and she says she will be able to come to speak to you or Rose very soon. Now you are wondering why she cannot come tonight. She has other duties, and also we have to fulfil ours according to plan. One thing she said was this: "Tell dear daddy that his words to the people are brought here, and some of the things he tells them are discussed among us because they happen to be of those things we have not learned of the Earth life."

This seems well-nigh impossible. Have I got this right?

There you go, you see. Now what do you think these dear angel children are, that you speak so? Do you not understand that the studies of those who came over here very young are mostly of the life and conditions of their new homeland, and that only little by little are they allowed to complete their knowledge of the Earth and its life which, nevertheless, has to be learned quite thoroughly as they proceed onward? So it is that every means is used, with discretion, to teach them. And what better or more likely way could you name than by enabling the father to be instructor of his own child? I am not going to say any more about that. It is enough. Think it over in a common sense way and you will perhaps come to a more enlightened frame of mind.

Well, but if what you say is true, one will be almost afraid to instruct one's people at all. And don't be cross.

Dear lad, no, I am not cross. But in you, at least, I have

been grateful to find a certain enlightenment as to the conditions of this life and their naturalness, and up crops one of those silly ideas of the nebulous order right in the midst of your mind.

You are quite right, however, to think that you should be careful how you give instruction. But this applies not only to you but to everyone; and to all thoughts and words and deeds of every one. They are all known here. One crumb of comfort you can take, however. You may be sure that when anything unworthy or base is thought or spoken, that is never allowed to find its way into such a sphere as that in which Ruby is. So make your mind easy there, my dear, and do not fear to speak out your mind; for silence is sometimes less welcome here than erroneous teaching, when that teaching is sincere.

And now, good night, and best love to you all. God bless you, dear lad, and keep you brave and true.

Tuesday, October 28, 1913.

Whatever we have been able to give you in these messages has been transmitted to you by means of impressing your mind with our thoughts and words. In doing this we take, and make use of, as much as we find there, so that we may the more easily get our own thoughts through.

Frequently, however, we have been obliged, of necessity, to call your spirit away from the Earth surroundings and give you a vision of the places we are describing, and you have written down what you have seen.

No, we did not actually take you out of your body, because you have been really conscious all the time. What we did was to engage and absorb your attention that we might infuse power into your interior sight—the sight of your spiritual body—and at those moments you were scarcely conscious of your surroundings. You forgot them and became oblivious to them, and then we were able to impart to you, in a measure, the power of distant vision; and to this we added the incidents as we had witnessed them ourselves.

For instance, when we described the coming of the Harp of Light to the City of Castrel we showed you the city as it is, but we reconstructed the incidents of the crowds on the walls, and the meeting outside the gates, and all the parts of the ceremony which we wished you to write down. That is what was done. How it was done you will understand some day when you come over here.[22]

We are now going to try to show you another scene. And here we may say that we use the word “try” because, although with a good subject we do not often fail, yet we are not omnipotent, and there are many things which may intervene to hinder our endeavour and modify our success.

Well then, give us your attention a while and we will tell you of a ceremony which we witnessed when a company of people came to visit our colony to learn about our work. You must understand that we go to each other’s Homes, and learn of one another in this way, and get to know what we can of the various aspects of work going on in different parts.

We were standing near the top of the hill behind this Home watching their coming. At last we saw them high in the air and far away over the wide spreading plain. The sky behind them was streaked with horizontal layers of crimson, gold and green; and by that we knew from what region they came, and the nature of their work. They were students in a distant settlement whose principal branch of knowledge was proper use of ceremonial and ritual, and its effects on those who use it.

We watched them coming along the heavenly way, and then a party of our own people, who were waiting on the plain, rose into the air and proceeded to meet the visitors. It was very interesting to see them meet in the air. High up in the heavens they approached each other, and when they were some little distance away our party sounded a welcome on what looked and sounded like post-horns, and then others produced other instruments and, while they played, others sang a welcome.

They had halted now and we saw that behind them was a chariot and two horses. It was very much like the chariots of old times. There is no reason why we should not use carriages of modern build; but shelter is unnecessary, and the old open vehicles have persisted to the present day.

When the visitors came near, they halted, and there the

---

[22] This is a very curious experience because it proves that what one may claim to have seen as a vision may well have been manipulated and indeed even created by others. I suspect this may explain some of the very odd events that people experiencing N.D.E's claim to have seen, such as Jesus with bloodied hands. G.J.C.

two parties faced each other, standing in the air. Try to imagine it. It seems strange to you, but one day you will see that it is quite natural to our present state, and, if progressed enough, we are able not only to stand but to kneel, lie or walk in the midst of space, very much as if it were on solid Earth.

Then the leader of our band and the Chief of the visitors approached each other between the two ranks. They took each other by both hands, and kissed each other on the forehead and cheeks. And then our leader took his visitor's left hand in his own right and led him towards the chariot, our party dividing to give them passage, and bowing respectfully as they passed. When the two Chiefs had entered the chariot their followers ran together with outstretched hands and gladly saluted one another as the others had done. And then all turned their faces towards us and came on at a leisurely walking pace until they descended at the foot of the hill.

I cannot make you see the effect of an approach by air. I have tried to do so more than once, but that is outside your imagination. So I can only tell you that it is most beautiful to watch. The movement of these high spirits, such as Castrel and Arnol and others of their rank, when walking on the ground, is not only most graceful, it is fascinating in its beauty of poise and movement. But in the air it is much more so. The soft, graceful, gliding motion, full of quiet and gentle dignity and of strength and power, is princely and angelic. So these two now came to us.

They descended, and then walked by a winding path to the Chief's house. He rules here with our Mother Angel, and I do not think there is much difference in their status or rank. For, except by direct questioning, which we hesitate to use, it is not easy to tell which of two people so nearly, if not quite, equal is the one who by a little degree excels. For so great is the love and harmony between such, that command and obedience seem to blend into one gracious and smiling endeavour of service, and we are at a loss sometimes to distinguish between the estate of two so highly developed as these.

The Chief's residence would very forcibly remind you of a mediaeval castle, set on a rock half-way up a mountain-side and surrounded by waving trees and foliage of many tints—green, red, brown and gold and multitudes of flowers and green patches of grass.

They passed under the gateway, and so within, and we saw them no more. But we noticed that the presence of that radiant company within illuminated the windows of the castle as if suddenly some thousands of electric lamps had been set going. And the coloured lights we saw were most beautiful, for they did not melt into one tint but mingled together, each preserving its own hue, and streaming through the apertures like so many streams of rainbow radiance.

I have often mentioned gateways, but you will have observed that I have not spoken of gates. Now, so far, I have not seen a gate to any of the many gateways I have seen here. You read in the Book of the Revelation of the Holy City and its gates, but I have thought of it, being reminded of it by these gates to what are, evidently, similar cities to that which St. John saw in Presence Form, and I doubt whether that city had gates to the gateways.

And that may be what he means when he says that the gates shall not be shut by day and—remembering that in the cities as he knew them on Earth, the gates were not shut by day except in times of war, but were shut by night continually—he adds, by way of explanation, that there is no night here in this land. These are only my thoughts, and may not be correct, but you can look up the passage and refresh your memory and decide for yourself.

I was not present at the festival within the Castle, so will not describe it, as I only heard of it at second hand, and prefer to tell you of things I myself have witnessed, which I can do more vividly. It was a most glorious affair, however, as one can well credit when so many high spirits brought their glory together.

Ah well, dear lad, you will see it all someday soon, when you and your dear ones will all be here in God's good land on which His love and blessing descend like dew upon sweet meadowlands, with the fragrance all around. And is it strange if we who learn continually how much more blessed it is to give than to receive, should seek to waft some of this sweetness on our breath through the Veil that those on your side may breathe it too and taste how sweet and gracious the Lord is, and how blessed are they who rest on Him? Whose blessing we invoke on you and yours, now and ever.

Amen.

Thursday, October 30, 1913

Place your hand against your head and you will notice that we are then able the more readily to speak to you so that you will be able to understand.

Like this?

Yes. It helps you and us, both.

How?

Because there is a stream of magnetism proceeding from us to you, and by doing as we have suggested it is not so quickly dissipated.

I don't understand a word of all this.

Maybe not. There are many things you have yet to learn, dear, and what we are saying now is one of those things, little in itself but still of account. It is often these small things which help to success.

Now, while we are not over anxious to explain the methods we employ in the transmission of these messages, because we can only make you understand imperfectly, still we may say this: the power we use is best described as magnetism, and by means of this the vibrations of our minds are directed on your own. Your hand being so placed serves as a kind of magnet and reservoir in one, and helps us. But we will not continue this, but get on to something we can better make clear to you.

In our life in the Summerland[23] we endeavour to help both those who come over to us and also their friends still on Earth. Indeed, the two phases of service are inseparable, for those who pass over here are often much distressed, and so unable to

---

[23] Summerland is the name given in many spiritualist circles to what is in effect the lowest "real" heaven. Below this the area is called the Borderland or the Twilight zone, and below that the Hells. In the numbering system used by both the Urantia Book and the Padgett Messages, Summerland is in the First sphere. However in other systems of counting, it is the Third sphere, because the Borderlands and the Hells are counted as spheres. In Volume Four further information is provided on the numbering system used in this series. As compared to the numbering where there are seven spirit spheres (called Mansion Worlds in the Urantia Book) and then the "Christ Spheres" begin; in the system used here each of these lower seven has been subdivided, making fourteen spirit spheres. G.J.C.

progress until they know that those they have left behind are being helped from this side. So we often make excursions to the Earth plane for this reason.

Last week we received a woman who had left a husband and three small children, and she begged to be allowed to go and see how they were managing at home. She was so anxious that at last we took her, and arrived at evening time just as they were all sitting down to supper. The man had just come in from work and he was going to have his meal before putting them to bed. They were two girls, aged about seven and five, and a little boy of two. They all sat round the table in the kitchen, a fairly comfortable room, and the father told the eldest girl to say grace. This is what she said, "God provide for us all, and mother, for Christ's sake. Amen."

The woman went round to the little one, and laid her hand on her hair and spoke to her, but could not make her hear. She was troubled at this, but we bade her wait and watch. By and by the girl spoke, after a long silence, during which she and her father had been thinking of the one who had passed away, and she said, "Dad, do you think mammy knows about us now, and Auntie Lizzie?"

"I don't know," he replied, "but I think she does, because I have felt very miserable the last few days, as if she was worrying about something; and it might be Auntie Lizzie."

"Well," said the child, "then don't let us go. Mrs.—— will look after baby, and I can help when I come home from school, and we shan't have to go then.

"Don't you want to go?" he said.

"I don't," answered the child. "Baby and Sissie would go, but I don't want to."

"Well, I'll think about it," he said. "So don't worry. I dare say we shall manage all right."

"And mother will help, and the angels," persisted the little girl, "because she can speak to them now, and they will help if she asks them."

Now, the father said nothing more; but we could see his mind, and read in it the thought that if this little child had such faith, he ought to have as much at least, and by and by he made up his mind to try the thing and see how it would work out. For the parting with his children was not to his mind, and he was very glad to find an excuse to keep them.

I cannot say that the mother obtained much comfort from her visit. But on our way back we told her that the faith of that child, if it was reinforced by that of the father, would form a powerful medium of help, or we were much mistaken.

On our return we reported all to our Mother Angel, and immediately measures were taken to ensure that the family should not be broken up, and the mother was bidden to strive to progress in order that she should be able to help also. Then a change came over her. She set to work in real earnest, and will soon be allowed to join parties on their journeys Earthward now and then, and to add her little mite to their stronger service.

But now we must leave that case for a time and tell you of another. A man came to our colony a short time ago who also had lately passed over. He was wandering about seeking somewhere to his mind, and thought this settlement looked something like what he wanted. You must not think he was alone. There accompanied him, but at a distance, a watcher who was ready to help when required. The man was one of those curious mixtures we sometimes get. There was considerable goodness and light in him, but that could not be used for furthering his development on account of its being checked and held in ward by other traits which he could not be brought to rearrange.

He was met on a path some distance away from the hill where our Home is by one of the workers in another Home, and the latter stopped and questioned him, for he noticed a strange and perplexed look in his face. When he stopped he received a signal from, the guardian, who was some distance away, and was informed of the problem, and so, all instantaneously, was equipped to deal with it. He spoke kindly, and the following conversation ensued.

A. You seem to be not very familiar with this region. Can I help you in any way?

B. I don’t think so, although it is kind of you to offer to do so.

A. Your difficulty is one which we might deal with here, but not so thoroughly as we would like to do.

B. I am afraid you don’t know what that difficulty is.

A. Well, partly, I think. You are perplexed because you have not met any of your friends here, and wonder why.

B. That is so, certainly.

A. But they have met you.

B. I have not seen them; and I have been wondering where I could find them. It seems so strange. I always thought that our friends were the first to meet us when we pass over, and I cannot understand it at all.

A. But they did meet you.

B. I didn't see any one I knew.

A. That is quite correct. They met you and you did not know them—would not know them.

B. I don't understand.

A. What I mean is this. When you came over here you were immediately taken charge of by your friends. But your heart, good in some respects and even enlightened, was hard and blindly obstinate in others. And this is the reason you did not recognize their presence.

The other looked long and doubtfully at his companion, and at last stammered out a question.

B. What is wrong with me, then? Everybody I meet is kind and happy, and yet I don't seem to be able to join any party, or to find my own proper place. What is wrong with me?

A. The first thing you must learn is that your opinions may not be correct. I'll tell you one which is at fault, to begin with. This world is not, as you are trying to imagine it, a place where people are all that is good or all that is evil. They are much as they are on Earth. Another thing is this: your wife, who came over here some years ago, is in a higher sphere than the one in which you will be placed when you have at length got the correct perspective of things. She was not mentally your equal in the Earth life, and is not so now. But you are on a lower plane than she is, on general lines and all things considered. That is the second thing you have to accept, and accept ex animo. You do not accept it, as I can see by your face. You will have to do so before you can advance. When you have done so, then you will probably be enabled to communicate with her. At present that is not possible.[24]3

---

[24] Mental capacity increases with spiritual advancement, but it appears that the wife has not yet progressed far enough to make up the deficit. This is the first instance I have come across where the conclusion is that one's mental capacity on arrival in spirit is no greater than it was before

The man's eyes became dimmed with tears, but he smiled rather sweetly and sadly as he quoted, "Sir, I perceive that you are a prophet."

A. Quite right; and that brings me to the third thing you will have to accept; and that is this. There is one watching over you always, always at hand to help you. He is a prophet, or rather a seer, like me; and it was he who put that saying into your mind to repeat to me.

Now the stranger's face became grave and thoughtful. He was trying to get the right and true view of things. He asked, "Is it vanity, then, that is my fault?"

A. Yes; but vanity of a rather difficult kind. In many things you are sweet and humble, and not without love, which is the greatest power of all. But there is a certain hardness in your mind rather than in your heart, which must be softened. You have got into a mental rut, and must get out of it and look farther afield, or you will go about like a blind man who can see—a contradiction and a paradox. There are some things you see clearly enough, and to others you are totally oblivious. Learn that to change your opinions in the face of evidence is not weakness or backsliding, but is the sign of an honest mind. I tell you this, further; had your heart been as hard as your mind you would not be wandering here in the fields of God's sunshine, but in darker regions yonder beyond those hills—far beyond them. Now I have explained, as well as I am able, your rather perplexing case, friend. The rest is for another to do.

B. Who?

A. The one I have already told you of; the one who has you in charge.

B. Where is he?

A. One minute, and he will be here.

The message was sent, and the guardian stood beside his charge, who, however, was unable to see him.

A. Well, he is here. Tell him what you want.

B. looked full of doubt and anxiety, and then said, "Tell me, my friend, if he is here why I cannot see him."

A. Because in that phase of your mind's activity you are blind. That is the first thing you have to realize. Do you believe me

---

death. G.J.C.

when I say you are, in some directions, blind?

B. I can see very well, and the things I see are fairly plain, and the country quite natural and beautiful. I am not blind in that respect. But I am beginning to think there may be other things just as real which I cannot see, but shall see some day perhaps, but——

A. Now, stop there, and leave the "but" alone. And now look, as I take your guide by the hand.

He then took the watching guide's right hand in his own, telling B. to look intently, and tell him if he saw anything. He could not be certain, however. He thought he saw some kind of transparent form which might or might not be real, but was by no means sure.

A. Then take his hand in yours. Take it from me.

The man held out his hand and took that of his guide from the hand of A., and burst into tears.

Had he not progressed so far as to make that action, he would not have seen his guide, nor have been able to feel his touch. The fact that he put out his hand at the command of A. showed that he had progressed during their conversation, and he immediately received his reward. The other held his hand in a firm grasp for some time, and all the while B. saw him and felt him more and more clearly. Then A. left them together. Soon B. would be able to hear, as well as see, his guardian, and no doubt he will go on now from strength to strength.

This will show you what difficult cases we sometimes have to deal with. Light and gross darkness, humility and hard, obstinate pride all mixed up together, and hard to separate or to treat successfully. But such problems are interesting, and, when mastered, give great joy to the workers.

Ruby[25] sends her love and this message to her parents, "Believe me, my darlings, the doing of a good and kind action, and the thinking and speaking of kind words by those we love on Earth are immediately telegraphed graphed here, and we use them to adorn our rooms, as Rene adorns her rooms with your flowers." God bless you, dear lad. Good-night.[26]5

---

[25] This message from Ruby seems to have reference to boxes of flowers we had been sending to our daughter, who was away at school.—G.V.O.

[26] With this last message the communication from Mr. Vale Owen's mother ceased and the messages were continued by a spirit entity

named Zabdiel. These are given in a further volume (2) of the The Life Beyond the Veil entitled The Highlands of Heaven. —H.W.E.

Chapter 6

Astriel's Messages[27]

The science of prayer—"Thy prayers are come up"—A present from the spiritual spheres—A lesson on light, vibration and gravitation—The lesson resumed—Orthodoxy and the Truth—Multiform service in the universe—Suns, systems and spheres of power—He giveth to His beloved during sleep—An example—Good-bye.

Tuesday, October 7, 1913.

BY the aid of others, who are with us now for the first time, we are going to try to give you a little instruction in the verities of the Faith as they appear to us on this side the Veil.

In regard to those truths which men have embodied in the Creeds we have little to say, for so much has been said already that, until much has been unsaid once again, men are ill-prepared to receive what we should have to say. We, therefore, prefer, for the present time, to leave you to look out for yourselves such truths as you find there, merely observing, as in passing, that all the articles are true if rightly interpreted.[28]

We would pass on, therefore, to speak of things of which men do not consider so much at the present time. These will engage their attention the more when they have finished their wrangling over aspects of the truth which, after all, are aspects merely, and not the fundamental truth itself. If they would

---

[27] See chapter 2.

[28] Depending on which books in the reading list the reader chooses, this will be found to be true, or apparently false. In the Anthony Borgia books, as an example, the spirit (Monsignor Robert Hugh Benson) has not yet, in my opinion, learned the true nature of many of the Bible's passages. If one reads the Robert James Lees trilogy, a great many Bible passages are shown to have Truth, albeit other than what is typically believed by orthodox Christians. In the Padgett Messages the same applies, although other passages are deemed to be altered and thus not capable of useful interpretation. On balance the statement here is more true than false. G.J.C.

endeavour to view things in a right proportion, then many of those matters which absorb so much of their time would stand to them as among the lesser things which matter little, and the,, would then be the better able to devote their attention to the deeper truths which are established here as well as with you on Earth.

One thing it may be well to notice is the efficacy of prayer and meditation. You have already received some instruction on this subject, and we would add to it.

Prayer is not merely the asking for something you wish to attain. It is much more than that, and, because it is so, it should receive more careful consideration than it has yet received. What you have to do in order to make prayer a power is to cast aside the temporal and fix your mind and spirit on the eternal. When you do that you find that many items you would have included in your prayer drop out from the very incongruity of their presence, and the greater and wider issues become to you the focus of your creative powers. For prayer is really creative, as the exercise of the will, as seen in our Lord's miracles, such as the Feeding of the Five Thousand. And when prayer is offered with this conviction then the object is created, and the prayer is answered. That is, the objective answers to the subjective in such a way that an actual creation has taken place.

This does not happen when the prayer is wrongly directed. Then the projection of the will glances off at a tangent, and the effect is only proportionate to the scattered rays by which the objective is touched. Also, when the prayer is mixed with motives unworthy it is proportionately weakened, and also meets with opposing or regulating wills on this side, as the case may require; and so the effect is not attained as desired.

Now, all this may sound rather vague, but it is by no means vague to us. For you must know that there are appointed guardians of prayer here whose duty it is to analyse and sift prayers offered by those on Earth, and separate them into divisions and departments, and pass them on to be examined by others, and dealt with according to their merit and power.

In order that this may be done perfectly, it is necessary that we study the vibrations of prayer as your scientists study the vibrations of sound and light. As they are able to analyse and separate and classify the rays of light, so are we able to deal with your prayers. And as there are light-rays with which they are confessedly unable to deal, so many prayers present to us those deeper tones which are beyond the range of our study and knowledge. These we pass on to those of higher grade, to be dealt with in their greater wisdom. And do not think that these latter are always found among the prayers of the wise. They are frequently found in the prayers of children, whose petitions and sighs are as carefully considered here as those of nations.

"Thy prayers and thine alms are come up for a memorial before God." You will remember these words spoken by the Angel to Cornelius. They are often passed over without being understood as the literal description of those prayers and alms as they appeared to that Angel, and were passed on, probably by himself and his fellow workers, into the higher realms. It is as if he had said, "Your prayers and alms came before my own committee, and were duly considered on their merits. We passed them as worthy, and have received notification from those Officers above us that they are of exceptional merit, and required a special treatment. Therefore I have been commissioned to come to you." We are trying to put the case as emphatically as we can in your language of official business in order to help you to understand as much as you may be able of the conditions here obtaining.

If you will examine other instances of prayer in the Bible in the light of the above, you may get some glimpses of the reality as seen by us here in our own land. And what applies to prayer also may be applied to the exercise of the will in directions not so legitimate. Hate and impurity and greed and other sins of the spirit and mind take on here a solidity which is not seen or realized in your sphere; and these also are dealt with according to their merits. And, alas, those who say that Angels cannot grieve, know little of our love for our brethren still battling on Earth. Could they see us dealing with some of these misusings of the Father's great gift they would probably love us more and exalt us less.

Now we will leave you to consider this matter further for yourself, if you think it worthwhile, and, as we see you are willing to continue somewhat, will touch on another matter which may be both of interest and of help to you.

On the top of your church tower there is a weather-vane in the form of a cock. You will call to mind that you yourself decided the form that this should take. Is not that so?

I had entirely forgotten it until you called it to mind. You are quite correct, however. The architect asked me about it, and I hesitated between a fish and a cock, and eventually decided on the latter. I am wondering, however, whatever you have to say of it.

No doubt. You see, these things are trifles to you; but there are few things which are trifles to us. Now, the fact that the likeness of a cock stands above your tower is the direct consequence of certain activities which took place in your mind five years ago. That is a case of creation. Many would smile at this, but we do not mind that, for we, too, are able to smile, and some of our smiles would perplex you, I assure you.

The meaning you had in your mind when your apparently not very important decision was made was that all might be reminded that St. Peter denied his Lord. I suppose you meant it as a caution against the repetition of such offence to-day. But you did not realize that that apparently trivial decision was registered here and dealt with quite seriously.

I must tell you that the building of a new church is an event which is the cause of much activity here. There are officers to be appointed to attend the services and guard the building, and a whole host of ministering spirits to be allotted to the different departments of duty in connection with a new place of worship. Your clairvoyant friends have been some of these already, but only a very few comparatively. Every detail is considered, not only in respect of the character of the minister and congregation and choir and so on; and the best among us, that is, the most suitable, chosen to help you according to the traits we observe; not only these things but the structure and all structural details are considered minutely, especially where symbolism enters in, for that has an importance not realized among you as it is with us. So it came about that the weather-vane was also considered, and I have chosen that because of its seeming triviality in order to show you that nothing is missed.

It was decided that, as the cock had been chosen in preference to other symbols, we would answer that choice, according to our custom, by giving to the church some appropriate offering in response. And that offering was the church bell, for which a choirboy collected the money. You had no bell when first your church was consecrated. The bird stood aloft, but could not utter his warning as his original had done to St. Peter. And so we gave him voice, and your bell to-day gives tongue—as it did to—night at evensong. And we are glad to see that he who chose the one makes the other speak day by day, for that is surely fitting.

Do you think we have our fancies here? Well perhaps that is so; and yet you were thankful for that bell, were you not, good friend?

We were indeed. And I thank you for your kind message. Might I know who you are, if you please?

We are spiritual ministers from a sphere where your own friends and mother have visited from time to time, and she told us of you and said how much she would like us to know you more nearly and, if possible, to give you some message. She and her friends come to us for instruction. Speaking for my own degree, some members of which are here with me, I would say that we have been glad to come and to know you. But we knew you and your church before your mother told us.

Thank you, sir, for your kindness. Would it be permissible for me to ask your own name?

Permission certainly, but I fear you would not know it, nor understand it.

Nevertheless, sir, tell me, if you will.

Astriel, who leaves you with his blessing. †[29]

Thursday, October 9, 1913.

We have come again at the request of your mother, and are glad to have this one more opportunity of speaking to you from this side. Never imagine that we are troubled to come to the Earth sphere, for although it does mean an experience of less brightness in environment than is our usual lot, yet the privilege counterbalances that and more.

Perhaps if we endeavour to enlighten you on the chemistry of the heavenly bodies it may be both interesting and helpful to you. We do not mean the physical aspect of the science, as understood by modern astronomical scientists, but the deeper study of their constitution.

Every star, as you know, is itself a centre of a system which comprises in itself not only the planets in revolution round the

[29] Astriel always concluded his communications with the sign of the Cross—H.W.E.

star, but also the particles of matter which suffuse that system, but are too sublimated to be cognized by any system of chemistry which is possible to those who dwell in physical bodies, and in their research are compelled to use both material instruments and material brains. These particles are between the purely material and spiritual, and indeed may be used both in the physical and the spiritual economics. For the two are merely two of many phases of one progressive economy, and act and react each on the other, like a sun and his planet.

Gravitation is applicable to these particles also on both sides, and it is by means of this force—as we will call it, as being a name you know, and also very little understood—that we cohere these particles together and are able, from time to time, so to clothe our spiritual bodies as to become visible to the photographic plate, and sometimes to the human eye. But we do more than this, and over a wider range. Were it not for these particles all space would be dark; that is, no light would be able to be transmitted from planet or sun or star to the Earth; for it is because of the reflection and refraction of these that the rays are visible. Not that they are transmitted, for their transmission and passage depend on other elements of which we will now say no more than this: It is not the rays of light, nor is it the so-called light-waves which are visible to the human eye, but their action on these minute particles which, on the impact of these rays, become visible as waves.

Your scientists have much to learn yet on this subject, and it is not our business to impart much which men can learn by the powers they possess. If we did so then the benefit derived from your Earth schooling would be materially lessened, and that is why we are careful to give you just so much as will help you onward without neutralizing the good effect of individual and collective endeavour. Bear this in mind, and it will then perhaps be seen to have a bearing on whatever we deem it advisable to explain to you in such messages as these.

The stars, then, send forth their light. But in order to send it forth they first must possess it themselves. And as they are not self-constituted personalities, in order that they may have it they must be given it. Who does this, and how is it done?

Now, of course, it is easy to answer "God, for He is the Source of everything." That is true enough, but, as you know, He employs His ministers, and these are without number, and each unit with an allotted task.

The stars receive their power of transmitting light from the presence of myriads of spiritual beings about them, all ordered and regulated in their spheres, and all working in conjunction. These have the stars in their charge, and it is from them that the energy proceeds which enables the star to do its appointed work.

What we want you to understand is that there is no such thing as blind or unconscious force in all God's Kingdom of Creation. Not a ray of light, not an impulse of heat, not an electrical wave proceeds from your sun, or any other star, but is the effect of a cause, and that cause is a conscious cause; it is the Will of some conscious being energizing in a certain and positive direction. These beings are of many grades and many species. They are not all of the same order, nor all of the same form. But their work is controlled by those above them, and these are controlled by powers of higher grade and sublimity still.

And so these great balls of matter, whether gaseous or liquid or solid, whether star or comet or Planet, are all held together, and their forces energized and given effect not by the operation of some mechanical law, but by conscious, live beings at the back of, and working through, those laws. We use the word "conscious" in preference to "intelligent," because the latter term would not accurately describe all the ministers of the Creator. As you understand the word, indeed, it would describe only a very limited number. And it may surprise you to know that those to whom you would apply the term are those which stand between the lower and the higher. For while the lower workers are not really beings of intelligence, the higher are more sublime than that term would imply.

Between the two there are spheres of beings who would bear describing as intelligent beings. Mark well that I am not speaking now in the terms we should use here, and which you will use when you come over here and have studied the conditions somewhat. I am using Earth language, and endeavouring to put the matter from your point of view.

Now you will, from what we have already written, be able to see how intimate is the relationship between spirit and matter, and when the other evening we spoke of your own church building and the allotting of guardians and workers, among other things, for the care of the material edifice, we were only telling you of the same principle at work on a minute scale. Nevertheless it is the same principle exactly. The scheme which provides for the upkeep of all those millions of suns and of their planets took note also of the rearrangement of certain jumbles of atoms—some in the form of stone, others wood or brick—which resulted in that new entity which you call a church. These are held together, each atom in its place, by the outflowing power of will. They are not placed there and left solitary. Were this done the building would soon crumble away and fall to pieces.

And now, in the light of what we have written, think of what people call "the difference of feeling" on entering a church, or a theatre, or a dwelling house, or any building. Each has its own suitable emanations, and these are in consequence of this same principle at work which we have tried to describe. It is spirit speaking to spirit—the spirits of the discarnate workers speaking, through the medium of the material particles and their arrangement and purpose, to the spirits of those who enter that place.

You grow tired, and we find it hard to impress you, so, with our blessing, we will leave you now, and, if you will, we shall come again. God be with you and your dear ones and your people, in all things and all days, Astriel. †

Thursday, October 16, 1913.

Should we perchance say aught that may seem strange and unreal of this our life in the spiritual spheres you will keep in mind that here are powers and conditions which on Earth are hidden from the outer knowledge of men. These powers are not altogether absent from your environment, but they are mostly deeper than the physical brain can bear to penetrate. They may be sensed or felt to a degree by the more spiritually developed—no more than this. For those who spiritually rise above the general level do touch the borders of those spheres which at present are supernormal to the average man. And no amount of mental capacity or knowledge can achieve this exaltation of spirit, for these things are spiritually discerned, and only thus.

We who are present with you this evening have come at the invitation of your mother once again to speak to you of our work and life as it is presented to us, and as we are privileged to know it. This so far as we are able. For the rest, we have told you of our limitations in transmission of such knowledge which, for this reason, must of necessity be incomplete.

Are you Astriel?

Astriel and other friends.

First, my brother, we give you greeting of love and peace in our common Saviour and Lord. He is here to us what He is there to you. But we understand now much which was not clear to us when we walked amidst the shadows on the Earth. And this we would say with all solemnity: let those who to-day amongst you are searching into the meaning of His Divinity, and the relation of that to His Humanity, do so fearlessly and reverently. For such are guided more than they know from these realms. And be it always in the mind of those who are sincere that they can do no irreverence to Him Who Himself is Truth in inquiring what the Truth is as He revealed it.

Nevertheless, friend, we tell you, with this same fearlessness, and with great reverence also, that what goes by the name of Orthodoxy among Christians in the Church on Earth is not a fair and true presentation, in many ways, of the Truth as we have come to know it here. Also we see among you too much unreadiness to go forward, and lack of courage and faith in the providence of God Who will, if men will follow, lead them more and more into the light, the radiant, glowing light, as it envelops those who are brave, to show them the right and holy way towards His Throne. Let such remember that that Throne shall be shared only by the brave who are strong to overcome come, and these are they who are valiant to do and dare, and pay the price at the hands of those their fellows who are less courageous and less enlightened.

Now we continue our instruction, and you will accept it so far as you can. What you do not feel able to receive leave, and perhaps, as you proceed on your way, you will find it fall into place little by little until you understand it all.

We were telling you formerly about the heavenly bodies and their correlation to each other. Now we will tell you somewhat of their creation and of the aspect they wear to us as viewed on their spiritual side. For you will understand that every star and planet, and everything material, has its spiritual counterpart. You do understand this, we know, and are going to build what we now have to say on that knowledge.

The heavenly bodies are the expression in matter, of ideas originating among those high in the Heavenly Spheres of Creative Power. They are all and each the effect of thoughts and impulses proceeding from those spheres. When a world is in process of creation those High Beings are constantly energizing, and projecting into the forming matter their spiritual influence and, so to speak, character. Thus, although the planets of your system are all conformable to one great scheme of unity, they are diverse in their individual characteristics. These characteristics answer to the characters of the Great Lords in Whose charge they severally are. Astronomers are correct when they say that certain of the elements which go to form the Earth are found in, say Mars and Jupiter, and in the Sun itself. But they would err if they should say that they are found in the same proportion, or in similar combination. Every planet differs in these things from its fellow, but all conform to the one broader scheme which governs them as a system. What is here said of the units which go to make up the Solar system may be applied to the wider range of things. Considering the Solar realm as a unit, it is not identical, either in composition of elements or in planetary constitution, with other systems. Each differs from its fellow also.

Now, we have explained the reason of this. It issues in the individual mind of the Chief Lord of the particular system. Under him are other great Lords who work in unison with his one governing idea. But these also have freedom in those things which are under their charge, and so on downward to the minute things of creation—the flowers and trees and animals and the formation of the face of the planet. It is on account of this latitude in creation and control that you have such diversity in detail; and because of the limit of restriction to the exercise of that free individuality that you have the unity which you find interpenetrating every department and sub department of creation.

Under these supervisors there are also myriads of lesser ministers of different grades downward until some of the lowest orders may scarcely be termed persons, for they merge into the lower species of life which you might term sensory, as distinguishing them from those who, like ourselves, are possessed not only of intelligence, but also of that independence in judgment which we know as freewill.

Are you speaking of fairies, pixies, and elementals generally, of which some writers tell us?

Yes, these are real things, and mostly benevolent; but they are far below the human sphere, and therefore are less known than the higher grades of ministry, such as the spirits of men, and those who have attained to angelic degree.

Now, a little more about the Earth itself. Geologists tell how some of the rocks are alluvial and others igneous in formation, and so on. But if you will carefully examine some of these you will find that they give off a certain vapour, or one might almost say magnetic influence. That is the effect of the original inspiration into them by those who formed them originally. And these characteristics are worthy of deeper study than they have hitherto received. The chemical composition has been, more or less, ascertained. But the more subtle influences proceeding from the ever-vibrating particles have been neglected. Yet when it is remembered that no piece of rock or stone is still, but that all its particles are in movement orderly and constant, it is only one step onward then to realize that, in order that this movement be maintained, there must be present some great force and, at the back of that force, a personality of which it is the expression.

This is true, and the baleful influence which some gems do exercise on those whose sentiments towards them are not governed aright, is an evidence of this. On the other hand, you have heard of lucky-stones, which is a phrase which shows some rather vague notion of the underlying truth. Eliminate all idea of chance from these matters, and substitute an orderly system of cause and effect, and remember the consequence of ignorance in traversing all natural law, and you will see that there may be something in what we have been trying to explain.

For the sake of emphasis we have limited our consideration to the mineral creation, but the same truth may be adapted to the vegetable and animal kingdoms also. Of this we will not speak tonight. What we, have said has been said with the object of showing that there is a field for those who have a scientific turn of mind, and who are not afraid to go farther afield than scientists have hitherto allowed themselves to go.

The whole may be summed up in a few words, if which be

accepted then the conclusion we have intimated must, of necessity, be accepted too. The whole material creation is nothing in itself and by itself. It is but the expression, on a lower plane, of personalities on higher planes, the effect of which their wills are the causes. As a man leaves the imprint of his character on his work day by day, so these great Creative Lords and their ministers have left the impress of their personality on these material phenomena.

Nothing is still, all moves continuously. This movement is controlled and orderly, and that is a warrant of the constant energizing of personality. As the lower grades of service are dependent on those higher Lords for their existence and continuance, so are these latter to those of grade more sublime, as these are to the One Supreme Energy, the Self-Existent One, Whose Will is our life, and Whose Wisdom is more wonderful than we can express in words or in thoughts. To Whom be reverence done from all who are in Him, and from us who, in the Christ our Lord and Saviour, dwell in Him, and He in us. Amen.†

Friday, October 24, 1913

We have come tonight with our friends, your mother and her companions, at their invitation once again, in order to speak to you some message of friendly help and counsel. And in thinking over what would most interest you, we concluded that if we were to say something to you of those powers which watch over the world, we might, perchance, be able to lead you, and those who are willing to follow with you, a little onward towards the great body of knowledge which awaits your searching when you have laid aside those trammels of the Earth life, and stand free to progress into the greater glories of the realm of spirit.

Who writes this, please?

We are they who came before, friend; Astriel, as you know me, and my fellow-workers of the Tenth Sphere of progress. Shall we proceed, then?

If you please; and I thank you for your courtesy in coming down here into this dim realm, as it must seem to you.

You say "coming down here," and that fairly well expresses the condition of things from your point of view. Yet not altogether, nor perfectly. For if the planet on which you live your present life is dependent in space, then "up" and "down" are terms which must be very restricted in their meaning. You already have noted this in your writing or, rather, you were impressed to note it.

When we said "the powers which watch over the world," we did not, of course, mean to localize these powers on one side of this planet, but to imply the all-enveloping watch which the heavenly powers keep about the sphere which is called Earth. These powers are resident in zones of which the Earth itself is the centre, and they lie in concentric circles around it. The inferior zones are those near the planet's surface, and progress in power and glory as the distance is increased. But yet, space must be enlarged in meaning when applied to these spheres; for distance has not the same obstructive sense to us as it has to you.

For instance, when I am in the Tenth of these zones,[30] my cognizance is limited, more or less, by that Tenth zone as to its outer or superior boundary. I may, on occasion and by permission, visit the Eleventh zone, or even go higher; but residence in those higher zones is not permitted me. On the other hand, the zones inferior to the Tenth are not impossible to me; for the zone in which I dwell, being a sphere, includes within itself, even geometrically considered, all the nine inferior spheres. So that we may, for the sake of clarity of understanding, put it thus: The Earth is the centre about which many spheres are; and is enclosed in all those spheres. And the residents in the Earth life are potentially in touch with all those spheres, and actually so in ratio to their altitude spiritually considered—spiritually, because these spheres are spiritual and not material.

Even the material Sphere of Earth is only so phenomenally, for it is a manifestation in matter of all these zones of spiritual power which envelop it; and of others, too, of other degree which interpenetrate it. Leave these latter aside, for the present at least, and consider the matter as we have described it.

You will now have some idea of what aspiration and prayer

---

[30] Astriel uses the term "zones" here not "spheres" but later seems to change his mind. This system of numbering has fourteen spirit spheres before the Christ Spheres are reached, where other books use seven. A short book outlining the major function of each of the seven spirit spheres (as numbered elsewhere) is called "Getting the Hell Out of Here" and is available at Amazon and Lulu. G.J.C.

and worship mean. They are the means of communion with the Creator and His High and Holy Ones Who (to put it in a way which you will understand) dwell in the highest, or outermost, of these spheres, and include within Himself and these all the zones within that highest Zone or Sphere.

And so the Earth is enveloped by, and included in and affected by the spiritual powers, of varying degree and kind, entrusted by the Creator—God—to all these ministers of all these spheres which are around it.[31]

But as you progress outward you come into a more complicated state of affairs. For not the Earth only but every planet in this Solar system has its like complement of spiritual zones or spheres. So, as you go farther and farther from the Earth, you come to a realm where the spheres of Earth and the nearest planet interweave with each other. As every planet is served with like attendance, so the complication is multiplied, and you will begin to see that the study of these spheres is not so simple as some good people among you evidently think it to be, who demand from us information as to the meaning of this thing.

Draw a diagram of the Solar system, with the Sun at its centre, and the planets roughly in their respective places around him. Then begin with Earth and encircle him with, say, a hundred circles. Do the same with Jupiter, Mars, Venus and the others, and treat the Sun in like manner; and you will have a faint idea of our work and its absorbing interest, but profound depths of meaning, who include in our studies that of the Spheres of God.

Nor have we yet reached the limit of our problem. For what applies to the Solar system must be applied also to that of every other star and its planets. Then each system having been separately considered, each and all must be studied in their correlation to the others. Think of it a while and you will acknowledge, I think, that there will be no lack of employment for

---

[31] This would appear to be enormously simplified. The Urantia Book has the most information on what happens beyond the Seventh Spirit Sphere - in the so called Christ Spheres. If consideration is given to the existence of untold numbers of other inhabited planets, each with their own Spirit Spheres, it is obvious this is too simple. The Urantia Book explains that the inhabited planets fall into seven groups of Super Universes, and that Paradise lies at the centre, but outside of these Super Universes. G.J.C.

your mental energies when you come over here.

Now, we are sometimes asked how many spheres there be. Well, having explained what we have above, I do not apprehend that we shall be asked that question by you. Did you ask it, we, who are only of the Tenth of these zones, would perforce have to answer: We do not know, and much doubt whether our answer to you would differ were you to put that question a million million of aeons hence, and we having progressed all the while.[32]

And now, friend and fellow spirit, we wish to ask you to consider one other aspect of this matter. We have said that these spheres are spheres of spiritual power. Now, two worlds affect each the other by means of that which your scientists name gravitation. Also, two spheres of spiritual power, coming into contact, cannot fail to act and counteract each on the other. Referring to your mental diagram of the Solar system you will see that Earth is, of necessity, acted on by a large number of spheres, and that the greater number of these are they which are those of the Sun and other planets.

Yes, friend, there is, after all, something in the astrological idea, and perhaps your scientists do well to give it a wide berth, for it may not be much understood by, and would probably be fraught with danger to, such as they who do not understand that spiritual power is spiritual power. It is real and tremendous, and every sphere of all these is reinforced or modified by the others. The study of these things should be approached with the utmost reverence and prayer, for these are realms where Angels of high estate go softly, and we of lesser estate look on and wonder after the Sublimity of that Being Who unifies all this in Himself, and Who has no Name that can be transmitted to us who only can reach out after Him a little way and then our arm is shortened; who only can see a little way and then the light beyond is darkness by reason of its intensity.

But we testify to you, friend, and those who will think reverently of things they cannot understand, that if wonder gives us pause time and again as we proceed, yet never do we lose that sense of a Presence Whose breathing is of Love, and Whose leading is as gentle as a mother's leading of her little child. So we,

---

[32] The Urantia Book answers this question, as it is a cosmology. See the recommended reading list at the end of this book. G.J.C.

as you do, take His hand and do not fear; and the music of the Spheres is around us as we go on from glory to the glory beyond. Come this way ever, our brother in Him. Never faint nor weary of the road, for the mists are thinning as you proceed, and the light strengthens into the further light which issues onward into the unknown, but never feared, so we tread gently and humbly, as little children do, amid the glories of the planets and the heavens of suns and spheres, and of the Love of God!

Friend and brother, we say good night to you, and thank you for enabling us in this our service. May it be of some help, however little or much, to few or many seeking after the truth. Good night once more, and be assured of our help in blessing. †

Saturday, October 25, 1913.

We will, if it is to your mind, continue our message of yesterday in regard to those spheres of power which affect the Earth.

Still concerning the Solar system, we say that, on considering what we have already said, you will see that we have not yet mentioned all the complications which enter into the study of these spheres. For not alone do the concentric circles of zones about all the planets and the sun commingle with all the rest, but also the relative combination is continually changing with the changing positions of these bodies and their consequent proximity to, or distance from, one another. So that it is quite literally correct to say that during no two seconds of time is the influence from them impinging on the surface of the Earth the same.

Nor is any combination of their influences identical in its effect or intensity all over the Earth at the same time, but differs in different localities. There must further be taken into our calculations the stream of radiation coming to this Solar system from the systems of the other stars. All these things have to be reckoned in, for bear still in mind that we are speaking of zones and spheres of spiritual beings whose powers are energizing continuously, and whose wakefulness never fails.

This, then, is a rough outline of the conditions which obtain among the planetary systems whose outer manifestation is visible to the eye and telescope of the astronomer. But what is thus observed is but a very little mite when compared with the whole.

It is but as a small shower of spray which besprinkles the voyager, as he stands in the prow of the vessel, and scatters itself in globules of mist around him. He sees the miniature globes of water where they float reflecting the light around them, and says they, are innumerable. But if this be so, then what of the ocean itself from whence they came, and of which they are, and to which they will return?

As that small cloud of spray-mist is to the ocean, so is the star-bemisted heaven, as seen from the surface of the Earth, to the whole. And as the depths of the ocean are to the eye of him who gazes over the vessel's side, so are the depths of space and all that it holds to the human intelligence.

Now let us think a little further afield. Space itself is but a term used to describe the indescribable. It is, therefore, without definite meaning. One of your poets began a poem on space and gave it up in despair. Wisely, for had he intended to do adequate justice to the theme he would have been compelled to continue that poem for ever.

For what is space, and where are the boundaries of it set? Is it illimitable? If so it has no centre. Where, then, is God His Dwelling Place? He is said to be at the Centre of all Creation. But what is Creation? A creation which has relation to space, or a creation which is invisible?

Now it is useless, for all practical purposes, to speculate on things we do not understand.[33] It is well to feel after these things sometimes in order that we may discover our own limitations. This done, let us now speak of such things as we, in a measure, are able to understand.

All these zones of which we have spoken are inhabited by beings according to their degree, who progress from one sphere to a higher as they accumulate knowledge within themselves. You will see from what we already have written that, as we advance from the lowest—to the higher spheres, there comes a region of spheres which are interplanetary, inasmuch as they embrace within their circumference more planets than one. Still advancing, we come to a state where the spheres are of such a diameter that

---

[33] The Urantia Book answers this question, and quite recently an amazing video has been created on YouTube that summarises this aspect. See the recommended reading list at the end of this book. G.J.C.

they are interstellar; that is, they embrace within their circumference not only more planets than one, but more stars, or suns, than one. All these are filled with beings, according to their degree of sublimity, of holiness and of power, whose influence extends to all, both spiritual and material, within the sphere to which they have attained. We have but advanced, you see, from planet to star, and from star to stars in their grouping. Beyond are spheres more awful still and more tremendous. But of these we in this Tenth Sphere know but little indeed, and nothing certain.

But you will be able faintly to realize, by a large effort of your imaginative powers, the meaning we had in mind when we wrote last evening of Him Whose Name is to us unknown and unknowable. So, when you worship the Creator, you have, I suppose, no very definite idea of the Order of Creator you intend. It is easy to say you mean the Creator of all. But what do you mean by all?

Now, know this—for this much, at least, we have progressed to know—that you do right to worship the Creator and Father of all, whatever you mean—if you mean anything definite by that very inclusive word. Still, your worship passes first into the lower spheres, and through them to the higher, and some worship goes farther and into higher spheres than other worship does, according to its worth and inherent power. And some goes very far indeed. Far above us is the Christ Sphere of glorious intensity of light and awful beauty. Your worship, then, proceeds to the Father through Him, that is, through the One Who came to Earth and manifested the Christ to men.

Now, all that we have said is true, yet it is truth expressed quite inadequately by reason of the limitations both of us who are speaking to you, and of your own Earth state. For you will understand that when we speak of proceeding through these spheres, we are really using phrasing of a local character, as of a journey from one locality through another to a third. And I fear, friend, that I can do little more at this present time than remind you that these states of which we have been thinking are rather better expressed as spheres than as zones. For, I would repeat, the higher include within themselves all the lower, and he who moves in any of them is present in all those inferior to his own. For which reason it is not without some degree of truth that we speak of Him Who is all, and in all, and throughout all; and of the Omnipresence of God.

Now, we feel that we have laboured this theme over long and should cease further endeavour to put into the little wineglass of Earth knowledge and wisdom to understand the vintage of these wide vineyards of the heavens. One thing is enough to know for you and us: The Husbandman and the Vinedresser, both, are sure in their power and in their wisdom to deal with us. Toward them is our journey set, and ours is to do the thing we find to hand, to do it thoroughly and well, and finish it quite, and then to reach out for the task set next in order. When that is finished well, then another will be awaiting us. We shall never find that we have reached the end, I think. For as me progresses one comes to feel the possibility more and more of a truth beneath those words "for evermore," "world without end." But we doubt if you do yet, friend, and we say this with courtesy.

And now we bless you, and leave you in the hope we may come again, for it is well, and there is sweetness in it, to bend to whisper into willing ears of some of the minor glories of our Heavenly Realms. Be sure, friend—and tell others who will hear it—that this life which awaits you is not a mere bodiless dream in a twilight region somewhere beyond the boundary of the real and actual. No; it is strenuous and intense, this life of ours. It is filled with service and endeavours crowned, one after another, with success; of patient pressing onward, and of indomitable wills attuned each to others in comrade service for the Lord of Love, Whose Life we sense and inspire, but Whom we do not see, and Whose Home is too sublime for us to know.

Onward we press, and often take the hand of one a little behind us, and with the other seize the skirt of one a little on before. And so we go, my brother; yes, and so do you, and others working with you. And if we are a little way on before, well, there are many who lag behind. Take their hand in your own, and gently, remembering your own comparative frailty, and if the task be too heavy for you, do not loose that hand you hold, but reach the other out—and here is mine and that of many another with us. You shall not fail, so you keep your own vision and your life both bright and pure. Nay, rather shall that Vision grow more glorious, for is it not written, friend, that such as are pure in heart shall SEE GOD?†

Friday, October, 31, 1913.

They who say that we come to Earth in order to help are correct. But they who hope that we shall help to such a degree that their own endeavours will be unnecessary are in error. It is not permitted to US so to enable you as to lessen the value of Earth's schooling. And although this seems so reasonable as to be almost of the nature of a truism, yet many there are who look to us to do what only they themselves can do; and that in no ordinary measure, but almost, as it were, miraculously.

Who is writing, please!

We are with your mother—Astriel and friends.

Thank you. I thought the wording was not quite like that of my mother and her companions.

No, I suppose it is not. Partly, of course, because we are of different character, different sphere, and also different sex, which is not without its peculiar characteristics here as with you. And partly, also, because we are of a different Earth period from your mother and her friends.

Do you mean you lived on Earth some considerable time ago?

Yes, friend, in England, when George the First was king, (1660 – 1727) and some of us earlier still.

About yourself, Astriel—who, I suppose, are the leader of your band—can you kindly tell me anything?

Certainly. But you do not realize that it is more confusing to give these Earth details than it might seem to you. I will say what I can, however. I lived in Warwick, and was a teacher in a school there—head master. I cannot give the exact year when I passed over here with any certainty unless I look it up, and it does not really signify.

Now shall we say what was in our minds? We are permitted to help, but with discretion. When people suppose that we ought to help them in scientific investigation, for instance, they surely forget that God has given them minds of their own to use in His service. And to that end they are left to tread their own natural way, and when they have done what they are able, we, now and again, point the way onward and help them to further knowledge.

Can you give me an instance in point?

I remember that once I was impressing a man who was investigating the laws of psychology in the matter of visions and dreams. He wanted to find out what was the cause of certain dreams being prophetic—the connection between the dream itself and the incident which it foreshadowed. He applied to me, and I told him that he must continue his investigations and use his own mind, and, if it were well, he would be given to understand.

That night I met him when he fell asleep and conducted him to one of our observatories where we experiment with the object of portraying, in visible form, the events hovering about the present moment; that is, events which have happened shortly before, and those which will happen shortly in the future. We were not able to go far back or far ahead at that particular establishment. That is done by those in the higher spheres.

We set the instruments in order and cast upon a screen a picture of the neighbourhood in which he lived, and told him to watch intently. One particular item was the entry into the town of some great personage with a large retinue. When the display was over he thanked us and we conducted him back to his Earth body again.

He awoke in the morning with a feeling that he had been in the company of certain men who had been experimenting in some branch of science, but could not recall what it had been about. But as he was going about his work that morning the face of the man he had seen in the procession came to his mind vividly, and he then remembered several scraps of his dream experience.

On opening a newspaper a few days afterwards he saw an intimation that a visit was projected to the town and district of this same personage. Then he began to reason things out for himself.

He did not remember the observatory, nor the screen pictures we had shown him, as such. But he did remember the face and the retinue. So he reasoned in this way: when our bodies sleep we ourselves, at least sometimes, go into the sphere of four dimensions. That fourth dimension is such as enables those who dwell there to see into the future. But coming back to this realm of three dimensions, we are not able to carry over with us all we have experienced when we ourselves have been in the realm of four. Yet we do manage to hold such items as are natural to this lower realm, such as the face of an Earth dweller and a retinue in procession.

The connection, then, between such a dream as foreseen and the events themselves is the relation of a state of four dimensions to a state of three. And the former, being of greater capacity than the latter, covers at any moment a wider range of view, as to time and sequence of events, than the latter can do.

Now, by such use of his own mental faculties he had arrived at as great an advance in knowledge as I could have given him direct; and by so doing he had also advanced in mental training and power. For although his conclusion was not such as would pass muster here without rectification in several points, yet it was roundly and broadly correct, and serviceable for a practical purpose intellectually. I could not have infused into him more than he had found out for himself.

This, then, is the method of our work, and, when people find fault with us and impatiently demand that this method should be altered to suit their ideas of what is the proper way, well, we have to leave them to themselves, and, when their minds are more humble and receptive, we return and continue.

And now, friend, let us tell you the immediate bearing of this on your own case. You sometimes wonder why we do not make these messages more vivid, as you put it, so that you may have no doubt or difficulty in believing that they come from us to you. Well now, think of it all in the light of the above, and you will see that, from time to time, you are given just so much as will help you to help yourself. Your training, remember, is still proceeding; you have not yet arrived, nor will you while you are in the Earth life. But if you go on trustfully and faithfully you will find that things will grow more plain. Accept what is not self-contradictory. Do not look out too much for proof or disproof; but rather for consistency in these messages. We do not give you too much, but we give you all that will help you. Be critical, certainly, but not unbalanced. There is much more truth than falsehood round about you and your life. Look out more for the truth and you will find it. Beware of the false, but not superstitiously afraid. When you take your way along a mountain-path your mind is alert in two directions—for the right and safe foothold, and against the unsafe places. Yet you give more attention to the positive than the negative; and rightly so, or you would go slow on your journey. So tread that you do not slip; but, go forward also fearlessly, for it is those who fear who lose their balance, and come most often to disaster.

God be with you, friend. His Presence is glorious here, and

shines through the mists which envelop the Earth, and that radiance may be seen by all—except the blind, and these cannot see.†

Note. —The reader will probably feel that the ending of this present series is somewhat abrupt. I felt so, too, and when at the next sitting Zabdiel[34] took up the tale I stated as much. On which the following conversation ensued:

What of the messages I have received from my mother and her friends? Are they, to cease? They are incomplete—there is no proper conclusion to them.

Yes; they will stand very well as they have been given to you. Remember, they were not meant to be in the form of a complete history, or novel. Scrappy they are, but not unhelpful to those who read with a right mind.

I confess I am rather disappointed at the ending. It is so abrupt, Lately something was said about publication. Is it your wish that they should go forth as they are?

That we leave to your own discretion. Personally I do not see why they should not. I may tell you, however, that this writing you have been doing lately, as all former writing you have received from us, is preparatory to a further advance—which I now propose to you.

That was all the satisfaction I obtained. So there seemed to be no alternative but to regard this instalment as a preliminary to further messages.

G.V.O.

[34] These messages were continued further. The second part was given by Zabdiel (of the same Sphere as Astriel), and is about as long as this first portion. It is published in Volume II of The Life Beyond the Veil, and is entitled The Highlands of Heaven.— H.W.E

Recommended Reading

Over a 15 year period I have discovered a great number of extremely valuable revelations from spirit. Anyone who decides to research spirit communications will discover there are literally hundreds of these, if not thousands. And there can be substantial differences between some of them. There are good reasons for this.

As a trivial example, accepting that humans do not change on passing through death, and accepting that there are literally thousands of opinions on life after death on this side of the veil, it's very clear that you need to be sure that you are reading the words of spirits who are honestly communicating what they have personally experienced, and are not speculating on things they have not experienced, but which are based on what they believe.

In the series to hand, Rev. George Vale Owen was very fortunate to have his mother on the other side, someone whom he could trust, and indeed her communications are always absolutely limited to that which she knows of. She then found others to come, of higher estate, and hence he was able to reach more advanced spirit beings.

The recommendations I make here are in similar vein to *The Life beyond the Veil*. None of course are identical, each has unique Truths to share, and some are undoubtedly more valuable than others. Some are certainly far more advanced in their teachings. All however can be obtained at low cost as Kindle ebooks and many as free pdfs.

The Padgett Messages.

These messages were received at the same time as *The Life beyond the Veil*, (TLBTV) but have remained in obscurity for many years, partially because they were only published from 1941 on, and took over 30 years to publish the fourth and last volume. These started similarly to TLBTV in that James Padgett sought to communicate with his deceased wife. His wife and his grandmother started the messages to later have higher spirits add their input. These were orchestrated by Jesus and his apostles and are typically of a more religious nature than TLBTV. However they also have significant details on life after death, and in particular the structure of the heavens, and the spiritual paths that are available. Most valuable of all is the careful explanation about what it means to be reborn of spirit, and how precisely to achieve that. This is experiential, not intellectual. You do not become reborn of spirit by learning anything. The messages are contained in four volumes, entitled *"True Gospel revealed Anew by Jesus"* and can be found on Amazon and Lulu as well as a number of websites.

The Judas Messages.

In 2001 a follower of the Padgett Messages started to receive messages from Judas Iscariot. Although not completed, these have a great deal on information on the life of Jesus as well as a number of spiritual topics. The book refers to the Padgett Messages and can be considered a progression of them. The book is entitled "Judas of Kerioth" and can be found on Amazon and Lulu as well as on the *New-Birth.net* web site.

Trilogy by Robert James Lees.

Robert James Lees completed three volumes, and these have some unique information. In these three volumes we follow a single spirit in his progression, and as a result they span 40 years. The volumes are: "Through the Mists" (1898), "The Life Elysian" (1905) and "The Gate of Heaven" (1931). The very title of this last book confirms the information in both the Padgett Messages and The Urantia Book that the heaven Jesus was talking about is not where spirits initially find themselves. The volumes can be found on Amazon and on the *New-Birth.net* web site.

Anthony Borgia and Monsignor Robert Hugh Benson.

Monsignor Robert Hugh Benson was first ordained as a Church of England cleric but converted to Catholicism and wrote many books. He was devastated to discover almost all his dogma was without any basis and set about communicating with Anthony Borgia who he had known as a child.

These books are some of the most detailed accounts of life after death. They are literally packed full of facts and remain probably the most informative available. Although the Monsignor had a lot to say about religious matters, he largely kept these comments to two of the six books. The books of a religious nature are: "Facts" (1946) and "More Light" (1947). The books covering the facts of life after death are: "Life in the World Unseen" (1954), "More about life in the World Unseen" (1956), "Heaven and Earth" (1948) and "Here and Hereafter" (1959). Some of these volumes can be found on Amazon, but all can be found on the *New-Birth.net* website.

Other Books.

There are a number of other valuable books on life after death that I have summarized on a single web page on the New-Birth.net website. This includes a very small book I wrote which can be considered a short summary of what we know about life after death. It is entitled: *"Getting the Hell Out of Here."*

Geoff Cutler. Sydney, Australia.